BOOKS BY HAL ROTH

Pathway in the Sky
Two on a Big Ocean
After 50,000 Miles
Two Against Cape Horn

Two Against

Cape Horn

Whisper

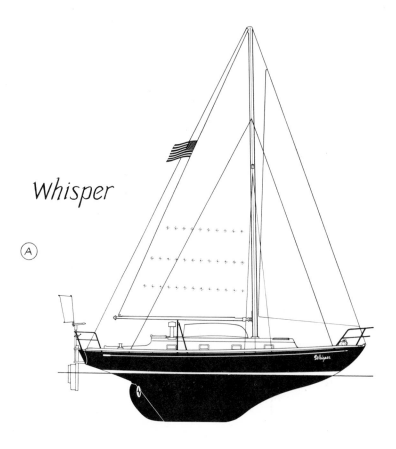

(A)

Length: 35 feet
Sailing tonnage: 8
Built in Vancouver, Canada

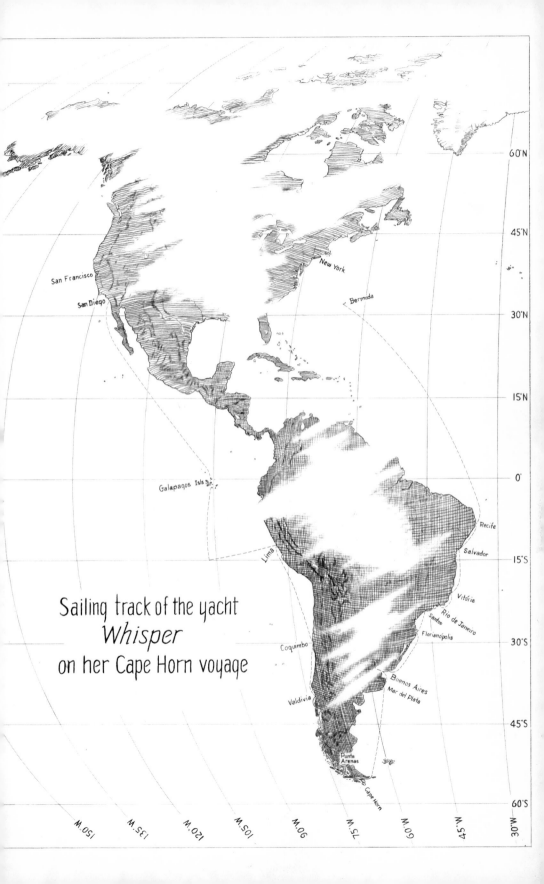

Sailing track of the yacht
Whisper
on her Cape Horn voyage

San Francisco
San Diego
New York
Bermuda
Galapagos Isls
Lima
Recife
Salvador
Vitória
Rio de Janeiro
Santos
Florianópolis
Coquimbo
Buenos Aires
Mar del Plata
Valdivia
Punta Arenas
Cape Horn

60°N
45°N
30°N
15°N
0°
15°S
30°S
45°S
60°S

150°W
135°W
120°W
105°W
90°W
75°W
60°W
45°W
30°W

HAL ROTH

*Two Against
Cape Horn*

W · W · NORTON & COMPANY · *NEW YORK* · *LONDON*

Photographs are by the author. Maps are by Sam F. Manning. This book is typeset in Linotype Caledonia and Monotype Caslon Oldstyle. Composition is by Fuller Typesetting of Lancaster. Printing and binding are by W. A. Krueger Co., Inc. Book design by Marjorie J. Flock.

FIRST EDITION

~~~~~~

PRECEDING PHOTOGRAPHS

The mountain world of the Chilean channels: an aerial view of Estero Reloncaví.

Looking north–northeastward from Caleta Voilier across the Northwest Arm of Canal Beagle on a winter afternoon toward the snowy peaks of Tierra del Fuego. Whisper (home port: San Francisco) is both firmly anchored and has lines ashore to strong points.

In the Chilean channels.

Cape Horn from the southwest.

Headed south near Cape Horn. This view looks back across the stern of Whisper *and northward toward the Wollaston Islands which are about twenty-five miles north of Cape Horn island. Vessels normally don't fly flags at sea (the flags wear out too quickly), but this was the special day when we sailed around the famous cape.*

~~~~~~

Library of Congress Cataloging in Publication Data
Roth, Hal.
    Two against Cape Horn.
    Includes bibliographical references and index.
    1. Whisper (Yacht)   2. Voyages and travels—
1951–   3. Roth, Margaret.   4. Roth, Hal.
I. Title.
G478.W46R67   1978   910'.45'0924   78–15466

ISBN 0 393 03223 X

1 2 3 4 5 6 7 8 9 0

*T*o all of my dear friends in Chile, and in particular to those who helped us after our misfortune:

Eduardo Allen
Horacio Balmelli
Isvaldo Benivente
Salvador Camelio
Fernando Camus
Hector Chavez
Juan Espinosa
Orlando Figuerola
Raul Ganga
Rafael Gonzales
Edwin and Jane Leslie
The crew of the PTF *Quidora*

Guillermo and Marina Herrera
Roberto Kelly
Jorge and Carmen Merino
Luis Ocampo
Jorge Piñeiro
Peter Samsing
Osvaldo Schwarzenberg
Oluf Torres
The crew of the *Castor*
The crew of the *Fuentealba*
The crew of the *Águila*

Contents

CONTENTS

Maps

*T*HE SEA is a mistress oft wanton and cruele,
Upon her bosom no man plays the fule;
And if he would her power conquest,
He must of himself give his true best.

—ANONYMOUS

ONE

Where Do Ideas Come From?

SOME fifteen years ago I read a book by W. A. Robinson entitled *To the Great Southern Sea,* an account of a voyage from Tahiti to the west coast of South America. Robinson had hoped to visit the thousand miles of fjords and waterways in the Chilean channels north of Cape Horn, so after crossing the eastern Pacific he sailed his big sixty-six-foot brigantine into the twenty-mile-wide channel of Boca del Guafo at 44° S, at the southern end of Chiloé Island. The weather was thick and the tidal streams were formidable. Robinson lacked suitable charts and tidal tables but he thought he could easily sail his powerful fifty-ton vessel into the sheltered waters behind the Chilean islands facing the Pacific. A strong tidal stream pouring westward out of Golfo Corcovado showed him how contrary the Chilean seas can be.[1]

"A sudden boiling millrace stopped us in our tracks," he wrote. At the same moment, black clouds swept in from the west. Robinson turned his ship to the northwest and fled out to sea.

The next day he tried to enter the channels at Canal Chacao, 120 miles to the north. Again the yacht was flung

seaward by water roaring westward from the inland waterways. With the barometer plummeting and squalls driving
down from thickening cloud banks in the west, Robinson
gave up his attempt to enter the channels in his own vessel
and sailed north into easier waters. Later he visited the
southern region on a local steamer.

Robinson's descriptions ("the glint of sun on snow-
peaks"), his delight with the country ("I was insidiously attracted"), and his feelings of excitement ("a glimpse of a
new frontier") all combined to give me a severe case of Cape
Horn fever—a contagion with which I was soon plainly in-
fected. My forehead was hot. My tongue was dry. I was
covered with spots.

In my mind's eye I could clearly see a shiny hull and
the white sails of a small vessel gliding quietly along the
dark waters of a narrow channel. Above the shore rose the
strong green of thick forests. Higher up, the trees became
brown-streaked granite spurs and cliffs as the mountains
climbed to thickening patches of snow and ice. Higher still,
at the top of the image, lay a splendid jumble of shadowy
glaciers, jagged summits, and swirling masses of clouds, all
of whose forms were softened by the blue of distance.

My dream was marvelous but it was only fantasy. I
would have to learn more facts.

I began to collect books about Cape Horn. I soon found
out that although there were a good many recollective sailing accounts by men who had gone around Cape Horn in
square-rigged ships (say from Australia to England), there
was little about Cape Horn itself and the lands and waterways to the north. I discovered that Pigafetta's famous account of the discovery of the Strait of Magellan ran to only a
disappointing 778 words and that most historical accounts
about Magellan finding his great waterway are utter fantasy
simply because no detailed records exist.[2]

My tiny collection of Cape Horn books grew slowly, two
or three volumes a year. The collection happened to be mentioned in the author's blurb on the book jacket of *Pathway*

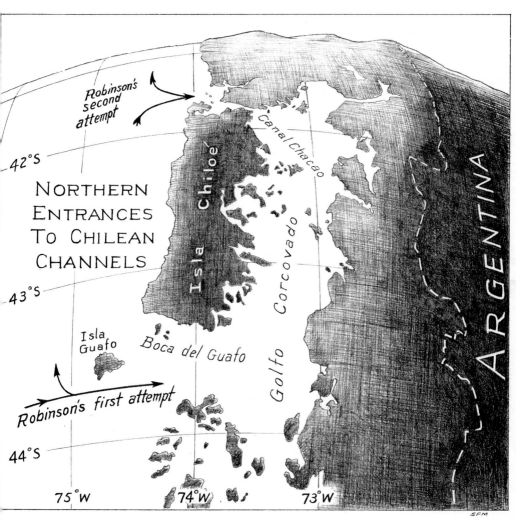

Robinson's
second
attempt

—42°S

NORTHERN
ENTRANCES
TO CHILEAN
CHANNELS

—43°S

Isla Chiloé

Canal Chacao

Golfo Corcovado

ARGENTINA

Isla
Guafo

Boca del Guafo

Robinson's first attempt

44°S

75°W   74°W   73°W

SFM

To Cape Horn
1,000 miles

in the Sky, a book I had written on mountaineering. Though the description clearly stated that I was merely collecting books on Cape Horn it was too late. The pregnancy had begun.

The book reviewers described me as a Cape Horn sailor, which was completely untrue. I had never been to South America. I had never gone near the Southern Ocean.

My friends were no better.

"When are you going to Cape Horn?" they chorused.

"Cape Horn? I'm only collecting books," I said.

"Ha! Don't kid us," they said. "When are you leaving?"

But year after year the Cape Horn notion persisted. It pulsed through my head like the penetrating clang of a church bell. Just as mountaineers dream of climbing in the Himalayas, sailors muse about Cape Horn. Some small ship sailors are horrified at the thought of going around Cape Horn in a tiny vessel. Others are fascinated by the idea. For them that cape of capes is a kind of altar, a Mecca, a place where a man is blooded, a symbol of adversity and achievement, of hardship and conquest.

The sailors of old complained and boasted about Cape Horn in the same breath, cursing the experience but loving it every minute because—like going off to war—it was the greatest adventure of their lives. A journey around Cape Horn was a trip to the ultimate classroom of the sea; the graduate was a deepwater sailor. No more needed to be said.

In the past, Cape Horn and the Strait of Magellan were the decisive marks between the world's two greatest oceans, and for four hundred years there was a mixed-up squabble for rights and sovereignty by Spain, Holland, France, England, and Germany—all of whom schemed and plotted, and who dispatched their best officers and ships to control this strategic southland.

In time, however, world trade became more important than sovereignty. Starting with the 1849 gold rush in California and continuing until World War I, manufacturing and international commerce expanded hugely. By the last two decades of the nineteenth century there were more than 10,000 deepwater sailing ships—5,000 British, 2,000 Norwegian, 1,200 French, 1,200 Swedish, and 1,000 German— almost ten million tons in 1895. Most of the ships were three- and four-masted vessels that carried a few passengers and cargoes such as case oil, coal, guano, manufactured goods, nitrates, rice, wheat, wood, or wool past the southern tips of Africa or America on their way to foreign terminals. These ships employed thousands of sailors, and it is from their records and writings and stories that the legend of Cape Horn arose.

The first steamship crossed the Atlantic in 1819, an idle curiosity with both paddle wheels and sails. By 1875, however, the compound engine and screw propeller were in full use and there were fifteen steamship companies engaged in transatlantic commerce alone. Steamships kept to precise schedules and sailed directly from port to port, made quick turn-arounds, and completed four ocean voyages a year while sailing vessels could do only one. The opening of the Suez Canal in 1869 suddenly halved the mileage between the Far East and Europe, and steam traffic through the new canal soon took the place of the sailing routes around the Cape of Good Hope. Nevertheless, the big Cape Horners which went from 3,500 to as much as 8,000 tons (27,000 square feet of sail up to 60,000 square feet) continued to operate profitably on long routes.

A large sailing commerce continued between Europe and Australia, and between Europe and the west coast of North and South America until the Panama Canal opened in 1914. This second transoceanic canal was the final fall of the axe for long-distance commercial sail, except for a marginal Finnish effort that hung on for another quarter of a century. In 1938 a dozen three- and four-masted barques loaded with Australian wheat paraded past Cape Horn on their way to Ireland. It was the end. By the time World War II began in the following year the perilous Cape Horn route was finished, a scrap of history at once remote and forgotten. Today only an infrequent giant oil tanker or a diesel-powered cargo ship rumbles past the black rock of the south. The albatrosses and the pintado petrels have the Southern Ocean almost entirely to themselves.[3]

Cape Horn remains a distant symbol of a vanished age when men drove their ships by harnessing the wind in folds of canvas. A relic of the past. Yet the lonely rock was a meaningful signpost to me. I wanted to sail around it. I wanted to try the Strait of Magellan. I wanted to see the waterways of Chile. My wife—Margaret—and I hoped to compare the Chilean channels with the fjords of Norway and the inside passages of Alaska. We had both read about the ragged Indians of the south and we wondered whether we would see any Alacalufes or Yaghans. A friend had told us that we would be able to sail in company with a splendid fleet of small sailing workboats on the east coast of Chiloé Island. We had heard tales about giant shellfish.

"Will we be able to sail close to the glaciers in Canal Beagle?" we asked one another.

"Will it be possible to see the great mass of Mount Sarmiento itself?" we wondered.

I had read so much about Cape Horn and the Strait of Magellan (Cabo Froward, Isla Tamar, Cabo Pilar) that I had to see these places for myself. I had heard (or imagined or fancied) that no sailor was a real sailor until he had tried the currents and winds down there. This was probably a lot of romantic balderdash but nonetheless it was a small factor.

We decided to go.

Margaret and I had already gone to many places in our thirty-five-foot yacht *Whisper*. She was designed as a stock racing-cruising sloop by the late John Brandlmayr and built by Spencer Boats, Ltd., of Vancouver, Canada. Her hull and deck were made of fiberglass. She had a lead keel, a spruce mast, and a small two-cylinder diesel auxiliary. We supplemented her normal rigging with an inner forestay and running backstays to strengthen the mast for additional security. Besides the usual sails, we carried a small staysail on the inner forestay and could easily run up a storm trysail which we kept permanently mounted at the bottom of its own track on the mast. These two small sails were handy when the wind was strong.

Over the years we had made dozens of improvements to *Whisper*, generally to strengthen her and to simplify the gear and to make the vessel more suitable for short-handed ocean cruising and living aboard. We had a windlass, four anchors, and lots of stout chain and lines. A self-steering device guided the yacht at sea and a powerful diesel stove warmed the cabin below. We had shelves of books, plenty of stores, and a radio to bring us music and time signals. *Whisper*'s cabin was comfortable, airy, and pleasant. Her only bad point was that she was burdened with perhaps four thousand pounds of cruising gear which put her low in the water. We fought a constant battle to take weight off the vessel.

(Overleaf) The interior of Whisper *as seen in a wide-angle photograph looking forward. In the foreground to port is the chart table. To starboard is the galley with hand pumps for fresh and salt water. The saloon has a table to starboard, and settee berths to port and starboard. Forward is the head compartment. Beyond that is the forepeak with two berths. Light at night comes from three kerosene lamps plus various twelve-volt reading lights as required. There are stout handrails at shoulder level on each side to grab when moving from one place to another. The cabin sole is teak as is the interior joinery. A six-foot bookshelf is above the port settee plus a three-foot athwartships shelf for large books on the forward bulkhead. Two additional six-foot bookshelves run fore-and-aft above the forepeak berths. At sea each person sleeps on a saloon berth or in the single quarter berth out of the photograph to port and aft. (The forepeak berths are suitable only for use in harbor.) Various bits of gear (barometer, fire extinguisher, spice rack) are dotted around the cabin, as are a few souvenirs from our travels. Four china dishes, two coffee mugs, and a crock of butter rest on the galley sink so we must be in a smooth and quiet anchorage.*

Whisper's specifications were:

overall length	*35 feet*
waterline length	*28 feet*
beam	*9 feet 6 inches*
draft	*5 feet 11 inches*
sail area	*527 square feet*
displacement (empty)	*12,000 pounds*
displacement (laden)	*16,000 pounds*

Our maximum speed through the water was 7.4 knots (or 178 nautical miles in twenty-four hours). Except for rare bursts, however, we never sailed at that speed in the ocean because normal sea conditions made the motion too uncomfortable. On a long passage we considered 100 to 135 miles per day as good runs. Some twenty-four-hour periods

were a great deal less, but we could generally count on 90 to 110 miles even in slow going.

Now *Whisper* was in California. We wanted to go to Cape Horn. We studied the charts, various volumes of sailing directions, and an enormous blue book entitled *Ocean Passages for the World*. At first we thought of sailing south to Panama, east to Trinidad, and then south along the coast of Brazil. However the contrary trade winds and powerful opposing currents looked too strong. We gave up the Caribbean plan and began to check the routes in the Pacific, the ocean that *Whisper* knew so well.

When you use the wind for power to travel on the world's oceans you soon learn that the long way between two points may be the easier, because fair or reaching winds (with following or beam seas) are kinder to the crew and mean less broken gear from bashing to windward. In addition, fair or reaching winds translate into faster sailing, so a long detour for favorable slants of wind is often the most prudent course. We could have sailed *Whisper* from California to Cape Horn via Tahiti (8,533 miles) which would have meant lengthy passages in the northeast and southeast trade winds and finally a voyage eastward in the westerlies of the Southern Ocean.

I liked sailing with the wind in the trades but I didn't want to make a long passage in the Southern Ocean in *Whisper*. I knew from the books of Smeeton and Moitessier and Knox-Johnston, and from my friends aboard the small yachts *Carronade* and *Manuma,* that the open wilderness of the Southern Ocean was not a good place for yachts—or even medium-sized ships for that matter. The odds are not on your side because the longer you sail in the Southern Ocean the greater are the chances that you will get into really heavy weather, that is, sustained storm force or hurricane winds. The winds, however, are not the problem. In a flat sea with plenty of room, a properly designed and handled yacht can survive almost any force of wind. The difficulty is the wind-driven seas which when heaped up and irregular

35

with cross seas can humble almost any vessel, large or small. The last thing I wanted was to get turned over and dismasted by a monster breaking wave which had grown and run unchecked before the strong westerly winds of the Southern Ocean for perhaps thousands of miles.

I knew from oceanographic studies that one wave in three hundred thousand waves was four times the height of the average. The English sailors of old never heard of oceanography but they knew all about *graybeards*, the name the sailors gave to giant waves. The Chileans called them *tigres*. The French sailors knew them as *les vagues énormes*. Regardless of their nationality, however, all sailors shook their heads at the mere mention of these dragons of the sea.

It was true that we would sail in the Southern Ocean from time to time during the trip to Cape Horn, but the more I minimized my exposure to this tempestuous place the better. Margaret and I had seen plenty of gales in the Gulf of Alaska, the Bering Sea, the Philippine Sea, and elsewhere on other voyages; nevertheless in the Cape Horn region the gale frequency was 26 percent in June and 15 percent in December. This meant that in the southern winter we would experience winds of thirty-four knots or more, one day in four. During the southern summer (starting in December) we might well find similar winds one day in seven. Of course these figures were averages; the weather could be much worse or infinitely better.

Quite aside from the clinical graphs of wind and weather, we had heard unnerving tales about the strength and power of the squalls—the sudden windstorms—which in the vicinity of the mountains of southern Chile were called *williwaws*.

In the end we rejected the route via Tahiti because of the long and uncertain passage in the Southern Ocean, and additionally because we didn't like the prospect of a fifty-day voyage from Tahiti. Twenty or thirty days at sea were acceptable but longer nonstop runs were not.

"I want to stop after a few weeks and see something," said Margaret. I could hardly ignore her urgings, for Margaret was a champion traveler who had gone from Bombay to England via the Suez Canal five times before she was eight years old and had never unpacked her suitcase since.

"If we harden in the sheets a bit we can go south via the Galápagos Islands and Peru," she said, pushing back her glasses and thrusting a forceful finger on a map of South America. "Then if we go south along the west coast we'll miss most of that stupid Southern Ocean."

From California to southern Chile was a hard business. We sailed to the Galápagos Islands (west of Ecuador), a

Once away from the immediate environment of land, we often saw pintado petrels, small sooty-brown birds that flitted about behind us, gliding, wheeling, skimming low over the water, and turning every which way to show off their white checkered mantles. These common petrels often follow ships for days and are also known as cape pigeons.

NORTH AMERICA

San Francisco

San Diego

New York

40°N

Miami

20°N

29 days

northeast trade wind

Galapagos

0°

21½ days

southeast trade wind

Lima

SOUTH AMERICA

20°S

Rio de Janeiro

17 days

Coquimbo

Buenos Aires

Humboldt Current

12 days

Valdivia

40°S

westerly winds

Cape Horn

120°W   100°W   80°W   40°W

SFM

passage of 2,947 miles in twenty-nine days, mostly to windward against the northeast trades which blew mostly from the east. We continued to Peru but the sailing was more difficult because the force of the contrary southeast trade wind was augmented with the north-flowing Humboldt Current. It took twenty-one and a half days and 1,956 miles to make Callao, the seaport of Lima.

We carried on southward in light and variable winds toward Coquimbo, Chile, which we reached after 1,610 miles and seventeen days. From Coquimbo south to Valdivia (929 miles and twelve sailing days) we entered our fourth weather system and found southwest winds that were sometimes fresh enough to oblige us to anchor behind a sheltering headland (or Isla Mocha in one case).

As usual, a trip at sea was a powerful lesson in geography. I had always assumed that the west coast of South America was roughly south of the west coast of the United States. I was astonished at how far *east* we had traveled. The longitude of our departure point in California was 117° W. Far to the south, we learned that Valdivia, Chile, was at 73° W, about the same longitude as New York. We had been obliged to make 2,640 miles of easting as we went south. We had had to slug it out to windward much of the time because we had discovered a lot of easterly wind in the trades. In spite of all my scheming we had experienced a good deal of uncomfortable sailing. We were quite ready for a change of wind.

To begin our Cape Horn adventure we had come 7,604 miles which had required eighty-one days of sailing, a showing of only ninety-four miles a day. To demonstrate the absurdity of toy sailboats, an ordinary jet aircraft could have made the same trip in twelve hours and at a cost of only two meals instead of almost two thousand hours of sailing and two hundred fifty meals! Nevertheless we now had our floating home less than two hundred miles from the northern entrance of the Chilean channels—an isolated and little-known archipelago almost at one end of the earth. On

The trip from California to the northern entrance
of the Chilean channels.

Ports	Mileage	Days	Months	Winds	Course	Notes
San Diego, Calif. (33° N), to Isla San Cristóbal, Galápagos (1° S)	2,947	29	December January	E 18–24	SSE	Much east in NE trades
Galápagos to Callao, Peru (12° S)	1,956	21½	March April	SE 18–24	SSW & ENE	Against SE trades and Humboldt Current (near coast); two long tacks
Callao to Coquimbo, Chile (30° S)	1,610	17	October November	S 8–14	WSW & ESE	Light winds and much tacking; against Humboldt Current
Coquimbo to Valdivia (40° S)	929	12	December	SW 20–35	SSE & WNW	Obliged to shelter at times
Valdivia to Canal Chacao (42° S)	162	1½	January	W 20–25	S	Good beam winds

7,604 miles in 81 days, or an average of 94 miles per day

board our little yacht we had everything we needed for a pleasant existence—our beds, favorite books, a writing table, and a few treasured possessions. The wind was free, food was simple and cheap, and we had a whole new world to explore.

TWO

A Change of Wind

A LITTLE before noon on December 31, Margaret and I sailed from the dock at Valdivia and glided down the eight miles of river that separated the city from the Pacific. The trip to, and now from Valdivia, a place of 91,000 people, was great fun, for along the river we had fresh beam winds blowing warm and fragrant from the bordering farmlands. We sailed rapidly and easily in perfectly smooth water, even passing a Chilean tug hauling two barges laden with cargo. Everybody waved and smiled while all concerned kept a nervous eye on the wind and on *Whisper*'s slowly increasing distance from the towline between the tug and the barges.

At the mouth of the river we slipped beyond the seaport of Corral and headed out into the Pacific whose familiar swells we soon felt. At five o'clock in the afternoon, the bearing of Punta Galera, the first headland southwest of Corral,

Here, nearing land, we steered carefully. The sea was rough and I wore my safety harness to keep me attached to the ship. The instrument with the white dial is a taffrail log which registers mileage. A life ring and a spare anchor hang on the stern pulpit. The strange-looking apparatus with the blue cloth at the upper left is a self-steering device which is excellent for use at sea where the wind is steady, but a good deal less helpful around mountains and cliffs and inland waterways where the wind is gusty and fickle.

43

bore 080° and we changed course to 185°, sailing almost south, with 115 miles to go to the Canal Chacao entrance of the channels. For the first time in thousands of miles we had a fresh westerly breeze and we drove through the approaching night with eased sheets. *Whisper* surged along splendidly without the miserable pounding that we had known so much since California. I felt free somehow—as if chains had been taken off my ankles.

The problem in sailing along a coast with an onshore wind is that if the wind blows up into a gale you have a dangerous shore on your lee side—a seaman's worst horror. On some coasts there are harbors or headlands or islands where you can find shelter, but on this part of the Chilean coast there were no real refuges. The only hope of a sailing vessel when hard on a lee shore is to claw off under reduced sail and to get far enough from land to be out of danger— say twenty-five to fifty miles or more. It is unusual, however, for winds to blow exactly at right angles to a shoreline which gives you a chance to work offshore easier by choosing the more favorable tack.

We had the hazard of the lee shore well in mind and I had chosen a course to take us twenty miles offshore. Fortunately, the barometer was high and steady and it was the season of best weather. In the early evening the wind increased to twenty knots, but instead of changing to a smaller headsail we let the yacht romp onward with the genoa because we had an appointment with a tidal stream.

We were quite aware that we had to pass through the entrance of Canal Chacao during slack water or with a favorable east-setting tidal stream. Our friend Captain Roberto Kelly of the Chilean navy had given us careful instructions when he had visited us further north.

"You must attempt Canal Chacao only when the conditions are favorable," he said. "Otherwise I think it will be impossible for a small yacht. The problem is that an enormous volume of water flows back and forth between Golfo de Ancud and the Pacific. Canal Chacao is narrow and the streams run hard. In addition, when the ebb, the west-going stream, meets the prevailing westerly swell, the result is an appalling sea—even for our large naval ships. When coming in you must arrange your program to be at the western entrance when the tidal stream is beginning to flood, that is, going eastward with you."

We followed Captain Kelly's advice and had worked out the proper hours. Now we were on schedule. *Whisper* made good time throughout the night. A few squalls passed over, one of which dumped a load of tiny hailstones on deck and obliged us to hand the headsail for a time. While the genoa was down I swapped it for the working jib. Margaret hoisted the smaller headsail at 0715, while I changed course to aim for the land to the eastward. Unfortunately, the morning sky was partially overcast; in any case, an early-morning sextant sight would have been useless for precise latitude, our chief concern. I tried my radio direction finder on the signal presumably sent out by the Punta Corona light station. The transmitted characteristics I received were the Morse letters OC instead of the letters CONA listed in the Chilean book of radio aids, which was only two weeks old. This meant I could place no reliance on the signal. As usual, when a bearing would have been handy, the RDF set was useless. Fortunately, however, I had no reason to doubt our dead reckoning plot based on the compass and the elapsed mileage indicator.

As the sun rose in front of us a little to the north, we steered southeast and ran before a twelve-knot westerly wind with maximum sail set again. Shearwaters and small black-browed albatrosses skimmed the water around us. At 1035 we saw a distant headland on the starboard bow. I knew the ocean depths were less because the westerly swell was increasing as it felt the floor of the sea. We busied ourselves trying to identify the land. The instructions in both the Admiralty and Chilean *Pilots*, our ever-useful volumes of sailing directions, warned of dangers to the north of the entrance, so we headed a little south to favor the southern

45

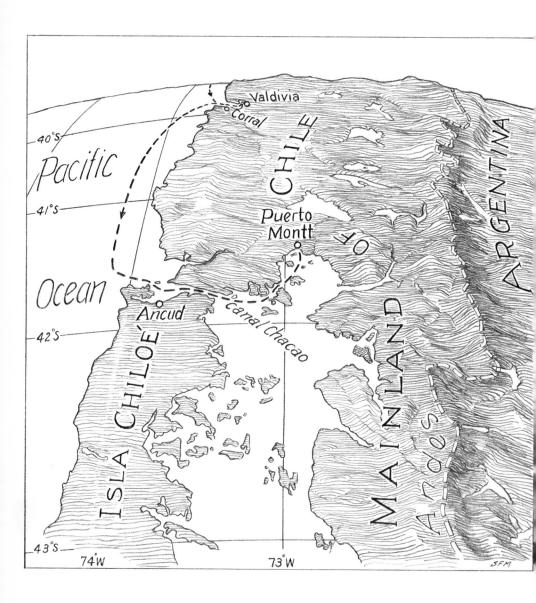

approaches. The key to the channel was the white tower of the Punta Corona light station, which we hoped to see shortly.

The ocean swells soon became enormous; there was no doubt about being in shoaler water. Sixty miles to the west the Pacific was 13,000 feet deep and extended in an unbroken sweep for thousands of miles—to Australia and beyond. The ground swell that we now felt was resonant, alive, and awesome. The yacht was bouncing all over the place in seas that were brittle and threatening to crumble; we had scarcely enough wind to keep the sails full.

All of a sudden I became aware of a thundering noise. Somewhere ahead the seas were exploding. As I peered nervously eastward from the top of a crest I could see mist and white water two or three miles in front of us. The great swells of the Southern Ocean were breaking on rocks.

The land appeared to be continuous to the right, so we eased off to port and gradually left the white water to starboard. The swells increased in steepness, and when we were down in the troughs we were quite becalmed and could see nothing except towering walls of gray water on all sides. Then up again for a look at the excitement toward the land. Margaret muttered something about taking a photograph but I had lost all interest in cameras. I wanted to get the hell out of there. My nerve ends were tied in knots and my stomach muscles were a mess.

I will never forget the force of those breaking swells. It was not a crashing waves-on-the-rocks-along-the-beach sort of action. It was a low-pitched boom, a vibration in the sea, a cataclysmic violence that I could easily feel from two miles away and which made the entire yacht tremble. The effect was a pulsing, a quivering, a wholesale shaking of the ocean, as if I were experiencing an earthquake or standing next to a warehouse of exploding dynamite. I was conscious of an enormous release of energy as thousands of tons of water were brutally halted at the edge of the continent. The angry water tried to continue onward and hurled itself into a froth of whitened fury. The forces in the Southern Ocean were truly astonishing.

Each transmitted shock of exploding water was enough to give any sailor palpitations of the heart. I had a momentary horror of being caught by one of those breaking monsters which would crush a large or small vessel like an elephant stepping on a peanut. I could almost feel a rippling of new grey hairs on the top of my head.

While I was edging away from the breaking shoal, Margaret was busy with the hand-bearing compass and the chart. She worked out that we had started to enter a small bay named Bahía Guapacho at the southern entrance to Canal Chacao. The breaking shoal was Rodal Guapacho. We took bearings of two small islets to the northeast which were in the right places, but we were unable to see the Punta Corona light tower which should have been in front of us. It wasn't until we passed into smoother water and went further east that we were able to pick out the hard-to-see tower, which needed a coat of paint and was quite inconspicuous—at least on the bearing we were on. For some unknown reason the light was on a point of land in back of Punta Guapacho, the obvious headland for the light.

In another hour we were behind the double projecting fingers of Punta Guapacho and Punta Corona. Here the water was calm, the tidal action insignificant, and we sailed slowly into a small cove named Puerto Inglés in Bahía de Ancud, well protected from the ravages of the Southern Ocean. When I let the anchor go, the sound of the chain rattling out echoed across the hills. A church overlooked us half a mile to the southwest. Green fields and patches of dark forests climbed to the uplands of Peninsula Lacui, the northwesternmost part of Chiloé Island. I could hardly believe the sight. We had arrived in the channels.

The little settlement of Ancud was five miles away to the southeast and I silently saluted the memory of the Norwegian singlehander Al Hansen, who had sailed through these waters from Buenos Aires via Cape Horn in 1934.

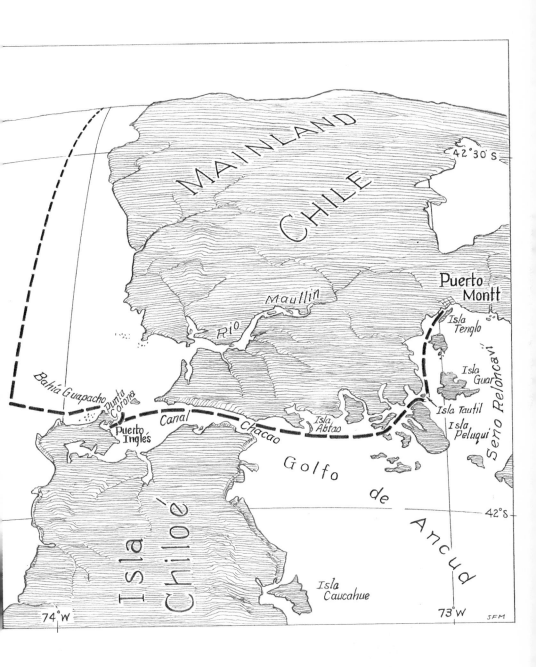

42°30′S

MAINLAND CHILE

Puerto Montt

Maullín

Río

Isla Tenglo

Bahía Guapacho

Punta Corona

Canal Chacao

Puerto Inglés

Isla Abtao

Isla Guar

Isla Tautil

Isla Peluqui

Seno Reloncaví

Golfo de Ancud

42°S

Isla Chiloé

Isla Caucahue

74°W

73°W

SFM

Hansen was the first small ship sailor to make the classic big ship passage from 50° S in the Atlantic to 50° S in the Pacific against the strong current and winds from the west.

He sailed an eleven-ton gaff-rigged pilot cutter named *Mary Jane* that was thirty-six feet long, with a beam of twelve and a half feet and a draft of six feet, designed and built by Colin Archer in Narvik, Norway, in 1904. The former lifesaving vessel of the Norwegian coast patrol was a double-ender, painted gray with light bulwarks and a dark rubbing strake. She had a pleasant sheer and was constructed of wooden planks fastened with hardwood pegs called trenails. Unlike most gaff rigs she was sailed without running backstays. The mast, however, was a colossal solid spar whose diameter at its base was half the width of a man's shoulders. *Mary Jane* had a reefing bowsprit that projected forward of the stem more than eleven feet; the vessel carried three tons of iron and stones for ballast. The area of her three flax sails totaled about nine hundred square feet. To balance the cutter for self-steering, Hansen adjusted the tiller with wooden pegs that could be pushed into a series of holes across the aft cockpit coaming. The yacht had no engine.

The Norwegian sailor was a good-looking, muscular man in his middle thirties with enormous hands and a shock of dark blond hair that tumbled across his forehead. He always sailed with a dog and a cat that he carried as mascots. He was especially proud of his library of a hundred books and of a large photograph of a bathing beauty contest that had been autographed by Miss France, Miss Germany, Miss Russia, Miss Rumania, Miss Hungary, and Miss Tunisia.

Hansen had been a sailor all his life and had worked as a pilot in the merchant marine. He had logged twenty-two thousand miles in *Mary Jane* when he set out for Cape Horn from Buenos Aires in February 1934. He was keen to get around the tip of South America and to Chile before April when the season of strong gales began. The long passage to

Ancud took him almost sixteen weeks, by the end of which *Mary Jane*'s sails were so ragged and patched and blown out that they were worthless. Hansen asked for new sails to be sent from Argentina.

In June 1934, almost at the opposite end of the world from his home in Forvik, Norway, he left for the port of Corral to the north. His vessel was wrecked in a violent storm along the coast and Hansen lost his life. No one knows the details except that some burned fragments of wood fastened with trenails were found. Now almost half a century later I thought of the death of this enthusiastic sailor— surrounded by his pets and books and his autographed pin-up picture—with regret. Hansen certainly belongs to the history of long distance ocean sailing in small vessels.[4]

Nothing can compare with the accomplishments of these solo sailors who—when the going is tough—have no choice but to carry on. The singlehanded ocean mariner is most assuredly the champion of all sportsmen and needs to be the master of a dozen disciplines, most of all himself. As a famous seaman once put it: "When they are tired there is no one to take their watch, when they are anxious there is no one to relieve them of their anxiety, when they think they are sick there is no one to laugh them out of it, when they are fearful there is no one to lend them courage, when they are undetermined there is no one to harden their resolve, and when they are cold there is no one to hand them a warm drink."[5]

The next morning we figured out compass courses and the bearings of different headlands and beacons to bypass the various shallow banks and rocks during the twenty-mile transit of Canal Chacao. We were so cautious that we laid out a course suitable for a squadron of battleships. The east-going tidal stream began at 1327; we left a little after 1200 to be at the right place at the best time.

What did we find? A light following wind, a clear sky, a

hot sun, and calm water. Our transit of the channel was so easy that I was a bit deflated after all the horror stories. We even took off our oilskins.

Now at last we were in the great archipelago of southern Chile, an inland sea of bays, inlets, waterways, fjords, gulfs, estuaries, and coves. Every sort of term was applicable because in a thousand miles of drowned mountain range the water assumed all possible forms. As we sailed east we began to see small islands which made position finding simplicity itself. We merely took compass bearings of three prominent land features in different directions and drew the bearings on the chart. The three lines crossed and made a point—or more usually a tiny triangle called a seaman's cocked hat. We were in the middle of the cocked hat.

The yacht Whisper *followed the Chilean channels and water-ways in the shadows of the Andes for 2,438 miles.*

While Margaret was steering I had been taking photographs, only to find when changing film that the camera had had no film in it. First I was mad at myself but soon I was laughing at my idiocy. We worked through a scattering of islands to the northeast on our way to Puerto Montt. The afternoon buildup of cumulus clouds brought rain showers, and the islands were first dark and then light as shafts of sunlight flickered through the moving clouds.

The countryside was hilly and dark green. Thick forests of low trees and bushes reached down to the water. Here and there stood solitary houses or small settlements with cleared fields outlined by wooden fences. The clapboard houses, generally unpainted, rose up tall and narrow with peaked roofs broken by smoking chimneys. We could see horses and cows, laundry on lines, and youngsters watching us. The country was like Norway except that the climate was softer and the slopes were easier.

The beaches on both sides of us were broad, of gravel or small stones, and were well marked with high water lines, for the considerable tidal action had scoured the shelving slopes into broad ribbons of seaside highways. Sheep and cattle patrolled these thoroughfares, chewing unknown fodder. We passed a church, and watched a black-hulled sailing vessel in the distance.

When the favorable tidal stream was about to turn we anchored in fifty feet of depth at Isla Tautil, not far from the first church that I had ever seen covered in brilliant pink paint. In the morning we continued northward, now in Seno Reloncaví, an inland gulf about twenty miles in diameter. To the east the sky was gorgeous, with several layers of marbled clouds—high cirrus, a pebbly layer at middle altitude, and ballooning cumulus at lower height. Bluish, snow-topped mountains seemed to rise directly from the eastern shore.

Ever alert for local knowledge, we followed a small passenger launch chugging along with people and a great mound of sacks of potatoes. From time to time the vessel, the *Chauquear* of Calbuco, would stop and a rowboat would shoot out from shore with a passenger and another sack of potatoes.

The harbor of Puerto Montt is formed by the protecting mass of Isla Tenglo, a skinny islet about three miles long, separated from the mainland by Canal Tenglo. As we neared the canal we passed several small shipyards, one of which was building a two-masted sailing ship whose image looked as if it should have been on a commemorative stamp or in a history book. We followed the canal to the main harbor which had very high docks along which lay an assortment of small cargo and naval ships. The tidal range was a problem so we threw our lines to the Chilean naval tender *Colo-Colo* whose crew lined the rail above us. We looked up at a row of black-topped heads with bright and curious eyes.

The interrogation that we had come to know so well in South America began. The questions, particularly the first, were always the same:

"When are you leaving?"

"Who knows? In a week or so."

"What was your last port?"

"Valdivia, with all the pretty girls."

"Where are you going?"

"Cabo de Hornos."

"How many on board?"

"Two."

"How much did the yacht cost?"

"The same as a small house."

"Do you like Chile?"

"Oh yes. Especially the beautiful mountains. And the Chilean red wines are very good."

"May we look at the yacht?"

"With pleasure. Tomorrow."

With a smile and a lot of handshaking we shouldered our way past the questioners and climbed up on the wharf to take our clearance papers to the officials.

THREE

A Rustle of Fabric

I LIKE to play a game with myself in which I carefully describe a place that I have never seen. I work it all out—the physical setting, sizes of things, people, what they do, colors, sounds, smells—everything. Then when I arrive at my unseen target I see how close I was. Sometimes my speculations are quite good, but with Puerto Montt I was a long way from an accurate description.

In truth this city of 80,000 was at the extreme north of the Chilean channels, nestled in the green foothills of the province of Llanquihue (lan-KEY-way) of which it was the capital. To the east and northeast a dozen high Andean mountains stabbed the sky with towering spurs of stone that were eternally frosted with white. Osorno was especially notable. It rose in a precise cone to 8,728 feet and loomed so close and huge above the sea that it somehow seemed artificial, almost as if a public relations firm had arranged for its presence. After each rain the surrounding peaks were dusted with a new layer of snow whose brilliance was often so silvery in the afternoon light that your eyes were hardly able to stand the glare.

The city had distilleries, flour mills, breweries, tanneries, wood product industries, and was a center for timber exports and sheep raising. People on holiday liked the nearby recreational lakes. In addition Puerto Montt was the southern terminus of the Chilean railroad system and—with few exceptions—the area marked the end of the national roads. To the south lay a wilderness of high mountains and thick forests, of isolated islands and intricate channels, of heavy rainfall and stormy winds. Isla Chiloé, to the immediate southwest, had a sizable population, but the numbers of people fell off abruptly further south. The only feasible transport in all this southern region was by water, and the shipping followed the natural waterways—called *canales* in Chile—which paralleled the north–south spine of the Andes for hundreds of miles. A half dozen small coasting ships handled cargo and passengers for the towns of Chiloé, for the hamlets of the mainland along the west slope of the Andes, and for the Chonos archipelago further south. Other ships brought limestone from Isla Madre de Dios south of Golfo Trinidad at 50° S. Some ships were on their way to

These oxen pull a cart laden with potatoes and farm produce through the streets of Puerto Montt. The stalls in the back sell baskets plaited by Chilote women.

*Skimming along
northeastward on a
fair flood tide with a
reaching wind from
the southeast, this
Chilote gaff sloop
slips along in the
shadow of Isla Tenglo
near Puerto Montt.*

and from the city of Punta Arenas on the Strait of Magellan. The Chilean navy had various patrol, work, and supply vessels. Finally, large cruise ships—generally painted a gleaming white with bright flags flying from every halyard and crammed with snapshooting tourists—occasionally stopped for a day.

With all these activities, a pleasant environment, and a reasonable climate, Puerto Montt was a lively little city. There were, however, other attractions.

As soon as we had entered Chile we were asked whether we ate food from the sea. "Do you eat shellfish?" was a question that we heard again and again. The Spanish word for shellfish is *mariscos,* and in Chile the word fairly rang through the air. In general the many varieties of *mariscos* were cheap and plentiful. Even the poorest man included shellfish in his diet.

Further north we had eaten scallops or *ostiones,* which were baked with butter and cheese and were so good that you immediately ordered more. We soon learned that the Chilean people ate *locos,* a kind of small abalone, as a first course with almost every meal. *Locos* were generally eaten cold with mayonnaise or a special sauce, were nourishing and quite filling, and had a smoky taste of the sea. *Choritos, cholgas,* and *choros* were mussels of different sizes which were eaten raw with lemon, fried, curried, or could be made into a hearty and aromatic soup. Clams were *almejas,* whose meat was fried or used for a thick and steaming chowder. *Langostinos* and *camarones* were small shrimp that were eaten uncooked with a spicy hot sauce or fried or concocted into a rich and filling broth. The orange parts from the insides of *erizos* or sea urchins were eaten raw with chopped onion and were considered to be the ultimate energy food for sexual power and longevity (always served by waiters with lots of sly and knowing winks). The *picoroco* was the giant barnacle, a five-inch stonelike crustacean—heavy as lead—that seemed to be of no use to man except maybe to be broken up in a rock crusher and used as paving gravel. Yet the center of the *picoroco* had a tasty white morsel of seafood—perhaps a cross between heart of palm and a chewy oyster—which you extracted and popped into your mouth. In addition there were *piures, machas, jaivas,* and so on and on, all sorts and shapes and colors of shellfish that were new to us.

These many creatures of the sea plus a dozen varieties of freshly caught ocean fish were sold at the market of Angelmó, which was on Canal Tenglo about a half mile from where *Whisper* was tied up. Angelmó was a functional place, strictly unfancy, and its stalls did a colossal business. Margaret and I often walked there to buy something to take back to the yacht for lunch or supper. The market was fascinating in the morning when the stalls were opening and the men were bringing in fresh seafood. Two husky fellows would hurry past, staggering under the weight of a pole from which hung a dozen great blue and silver mackerel, still glistening with sea water. A shout from behind would clear people to the sides as a wheelbarrow load of fresh

The food staple and delight of the Chileans in the south are shellfish. Here we see palm-sized mussels which are a main food-stuff and occur naturally by the millions.

clams was rushed along the walkway and dumped with a clatter of shells at a stallkeeper's feet. Perspiring men carried heavy boxes of *congrio colorado*, Chile's tastiest fish, to the counters where the big congers were fileted and exhibited and snapped up by housewives who couldn't wait to get the fish into their string shopping bags. Sure-footed boys brought in boxes of prickly sea urchins, beautifully packed in neat rows like hen's eggs. The boxes were handled as carefully as new babies in order not to break the delicate shells until a professional opener deftly cracked the sea urchins and extracted the orange meat just before selling it.

The smells of the market were sharp and pungent and pricked at my nose like the offerings of a spice market. Never had my nostrils been assaulted by such aromas. Something undefinable told me at once of the wholesome power in these seafoods. I was repelled and attracted at the same moment.

The sellers in the stalls were a confident and cocky lot of fat, merry, and ribald entrepreneurs who would crack open a shellfish, give you a taste, and then double up with laughter watching your face as you sampled something you had never tasted before.

The seafood market at Angelmó, however, was only half its business. The tiny bay was a gently sloping drying harbor that was safe in all weather. We were amazed to discover that over three hundred small commercial sailing vessels from the extensive waters around Chiloé, the Cordillera, and the surrounding islands came to trade.

The little ships were all single-masted cargo carriers from twenty-eight to forty-five feet long that were sailed in protected waters in sight of land. The black-tarred hulls had a beam of some 50 percent of the overall length, sharply flaring topsides, long keels, and almost flat bottoms which enabled them to be easily run aground and to lie at shallow angles when the tide was out.

Most were identical in design, with transom sterns and outboard rudders, and were rigged as gaff sloops with small jibs tacked to the ends of short bowsprits. The wooden hulls were carvel planked with *ciprés* which was copper fastened. Round beach stones made up the ballast. The anchor warps were braided from a tough local vine called *peta;* the parrel hoops around the mast to hold the hand-sewn canvas sails were formed of circlets of a native vine called *quilineja.*

The workboats had no engines, no lights, no compasses— nothing complicated to get out of order. The idea was to move cargo and people at low cost. Sails, oars, and the skills of the sailors were quite enough. I had the feeling that this commerce had gone on for ages and would continue long after automobiles, airplanes, and atomic bombs were forgotten. Indeed except for an occasional piece of synthetic line there was nothing of the twentieth century on these vessels at all.

The little Chilote ships came laden with colossal loads of firewood, bags of potatoes, sacks of wheat, and heavy boxes of shellfish. With high flush decks and the entire inside of the hull given to stowage, the carrying capacity of the small ships was unbelievable. In addition, the decks were often piled high with lumber, scrap boards, empty demijohns for wine, and three or four miserable sheep. The island women sometimes wove great stacks of shopping baskets to sell at the market and neat piles of them were sandwiched into odd corners on the deck. The upshot of all the bulky deck cargo was that the poor helmsman often had to stand tall and erect and to peer around things in order to see where he was going.

Besides the cargo were the owner, a sailor or two, plus various wives, girl friends, children, relatives with enormous suitcases, and sailing acquaintances. Cooking took place on deck over a large, three-legged black iron pan in which a wood fire was kindled. An iron grill over the fire held a kettle and a cooking pot.

A trip to Puerto Montt was not only for business but provided a social and shopping excursion as well. When a *lancha Chilote a vela* came in you could hear the excited chatter of the people on the boat carrying over the water. The children would be laughing and jumping about and all

Here are eight of the fleet of three hundred sailing vessels that take care of commerce around Isla Chiloé, the Cordillera, and Puerto Montt. With their

black-tarred wooden hulls, single masts, and highly peaked gaff mainsails, the
little ships are distinctive and unique.

on board were anxious to get landed and see their friends who were waving from the shore.

The sailors of these cargo vessels worked the strong tides masterfully, sometimes anchoring during foul tides. If the weather was bad the captain sought shelter in any one of a dozen handy coves or he nipped around to the lee of a nearby island. If this wasn't possible, he simply ran his boat ashore. With smooth water, an ebb tide, and a weather shore, the ship—like that of Ulysses—was soon high and dry and safe. The lack of a compass wasn't serious because the sailing routes were well known and the helmsman usually had a few familiar islands or mountains in sight.

In a calm a couple of long oars appeared and the people took turns rowing or sculling. When a boat came into the shallow waters of Angelmó she was poled near the shore until she was aground close to her neighbors. A rusty anchor was tossed into the mud. Usually twelve or fifteen gaff sloops were in the harbor at one time. They stayed two or three days, did their business, and then slipped out quietly at the beginning of high water.

These small cargo vessels were unloaded by the owners and helpers who threw the goods into two-wheeled horse-drawn freight carts that were backed alongside the hulls. Often four or five carts worked at a single ship, the horses

A trip to market is a wonderful family outing. Here a man and his wife and their seven children glide southwestward along Canal Tenglo toward home after a visit to market to drop off island produce and pick up a few necessities. Junior steers while father pauses at an oar. Mother, in the bow, fondles a young child. This vessel is a double-ender—less common—and has been fastened with iron nails, now bleeding and streaking the topsides with rust. The sails are enough to make a yachtsman weep, but seem adequate for this family workboat.

(Overleaf) At low water in the drying harbor of Angelmó, eleven sailing sloops rest on one side of their hulls and prepare to unload cargo from their home ports.

wading in belly-deep water while being jockeyed into position by expert draymen who snapped their whips and shouted friendly curses at their plodding charges. The cargo was handed or tossed into the carts which went back and forth to shore like water beetles.

Horse carts easily work around the grounded sailing fleet, taking firewood, potatoes, and sheep, and returning with sacks of flour and sugar. The entire interior of the vessels is for cargo so the crews live on deck, cooking over little wooden fires that are set in three-legged iron braziers. Arrival time is a great chance to see friends and exchange information and gossip, so the crew do a lot of socializing.

We listened to the squeak of the carts' wheels, the splashing of the horses, and the banging of the sticks of firewood against the sides of the carts. We heard the squawking of swallowtail gulls on the alert for food and the yells of the men from one boat to another. We smelled horses and sea-weed and freshly sawn lumber. We inhaled aromas of dried fish and potatoes and onions as grunting men carried loads past us.

All these sounds and smells mixed with the movements of the people and animals and birds and water. These impressions merged further with the colors and forms of the masts and sails and hulls of the grounded fleet. We heard the babble of fish buyers, the lament of sellers, the screaming of children, and the gossip of women. A grand scene had exploded before us; it was a true opera of life, complete with comedians, martyrs, self-proclaimed tycoons, city slickers, country rubes, heroes, and fools. We never got tired of watching.

When Margaret and I walked back to *Whisper* we heard the clip-clop of horses' hooves on the bricks of the waterfront streets. Sometimes we saw oxen in front of wagons of farm produce. At the docks the gondola railroad cars filled with limestone were pulled by small locomotives freshly painted black and neatly trimmed with red. Their whistles screamed through the air, and the coal smoke rose from their stacks in widening swaths of black that looked glossy and hard against the satin white of the distant mountains.

Puerto Montt was a good place to stock up on food for the trip to Cape Horn. We had no idea what we would find on Chiloé Island or further south. Experience had taught us that when we saw something we needed we should buy it at once because we probably would not find it again. We already had many food stores on board. Margaret topped up her supplies of flour, sugar, cooking oil, potatoes, and onions, plus the usual fresh food. We had bought plenty of canned goods in Peru.

Whisper was in good order except that the compass was suspect. We had had the instrument adjusted by a professional in California and it worked perfectly as far as northern Chile, where we began to get too far offshore on some of our coastal hops. I took azimuths of the sun and discovered that we had a significant error. Since we were now tied up to a naval ship with a professional navigator on board I asked the lieutenant to help us.

There were half a dozen precisely placed buoys and towers in the harbor area so the navigator went out with us and constructed a deviation curve for the compass. While I was turning one of the adjustable magnets at the bottom of the compass, however, the whole built-in adjustment system fell to pieces, another casualty of red brass and salt water. Upon looking into the system I found that one of the adjustment magnets was loose and rolling around. No wonder we had had problems! I made a twenty-eight–dollar telephone call to the makers, E. S. Ritchie of Pembroke, Massachusetts, who airmailed new parts. Unfortunately, they—like other packages in southern Chile—never arrived. I finally junked the entire correction system and swung the compass without the correctors. I learned to verify the new deviation chart by checking the compass whenever I got between two points of land that were accurately charted.

The crews of the various commercial cargo ships heading south were forever trying out their lifeboats in Canal Tenglo. The boats were sturdy and well built, with flotation tanks and water breakers. The trials were serious business and the coxwains tolerated no fooling around. The orange-painted boats not only had small diesel engines and sailing rigs, but they had great bundles of long oars. I was astonished at how well the men used the oars. All these preparations of lifeboats and emergency equipment were a bit upsetting. When I mentioned where *Whisper* was bound, the eyeballs of our listeners invariably turned toward heaven and the people crossed themselves.

All vessels traveling through the Chilean channels were required to have a pilot. We had asked for an exemption because we would be traveling by day only and had a full set of charts—ninety or so—plus four volumes of detailed sailing directions. We told the authorities where we were going and gave them an approximate schedule. We were requested to report at several places on the way and to stay in the main channels ("No exploring, please").

We asked the local naval commander, Osvaldo Schwarzenberg, and Luis Macias, the captain of the Chilean naval tender *Lautaro,* for their advice about several alternate routes and about anchorages in general. One afternoon we spread out an armload of charts which the two officers were kind enough to mark with cautions, favorite anchorages, good watering places, and friends' names.

"You will find three places with very dirty weather," said Comandante Schwarzenberg. "Golfo de Penas, Isla Tamar, and Cabo Froward. I suggest that you have a good rest before you try those areas. Also you should rub your favorite rabbit's foot and get what help you can from up there," he said, looking upward while making the usual gestures toward heaven.

Puerto Montt had a tiny yacht club with a few power launches and sailing dinghies. The sole cruising yacht was a small ketch with red sails named *Odin* that was owned by Guillermo and Marina Herrera. Willi and Mari, as they were called, became good friends and we often ate at their home on the hill above the city. The Herreras were good prospects for the sailing life because they kept their little house as neat as a ship, with everything tidy and perfectly in place. Willi and Mari took us for drives to see the lakes north of Puerto Montt. They suggested that we move *Whisper* from the congested environment of the docks to an anchorage at the yacht club about two miles southwest on Canal Tenglo.

We found the anchorage quiet and pleasant and near a local bus line so we could ride into Puerto Montt. In South America most people don't have automobiles so the bus transport is highly developed. There are lots of small buses, they run frequently, and go everywhere for trifling fares. The buses—bouncing along and often smoking frightfully—move quickly because the drivers make it a point of honor to race from stop to stop at full throttle.

We didn't like the Puerto Montt museum, but we saw a wonderful private museum dedicated to early life on Chiloé Island. The owner and curator was an author and woodcarver named Narciso Garcia, who had assembled a superb collection of historical artifacts. Most museums are dullsville, but Garcia's collections were grouped to give surprising insights into the island life of a century ago. Garcia gave us a good tour and even with the language problem had us laughing or astonished in turn. The Chilote people of generations past had curious ways. On wash day, for example, a woman put her dirty clothes into a large wooden tub on the ground. She added soap and water and then climbed into the tub and trod on the wash with her bare feet to agitate and clean the clothes. In one room we saw tools and plumbing parts and farm implements—even complex threaded parts—that were constructed almost entirely from wood. Garcia's wife was hard at work on a definitive Chilote dictionary. Certainly the worthwhile work of this energetic couple should qualify them for assistance from the Chilean government.

One morning I watched an enormous Mercedes bus try to turn a corner into a narrow street in downtown Puerto Montt. The driver saw that it was hopeless so he stopped and backed and filled and backed and filled. Behind him was a horse pulling a milk delivery cart. The horse and cart were small; the bus was very much larger. I watched the pleasant sight of the bus being stuck while the horse nimbly slipped around and went on about his business.

The following night when we were on *Whisper* I saw a mouse in the forepeak. The creature had probably gotten on board when we were at the commercial docks. The mouse was playing among some newspapers—perhaps building a nest. I got out a trap, cocked the spring, and baited the trigger with cheese. Later I happened to mention the mouse to Willi Herrera who was on board at the time.

"We have a mouse on board," I said.

Willi shook his head. "Oh no," he replied. "You are mistaken. Mice never come to yachts. I am positive of that. Besides I—"

At that instant there was a sharp snap from the forepeak. I rushed forward and returned holding the trap from which the mouse dangled. Willi was dumfounded.

It was pleasant in Canal Tenglo. We had never been anchored in an area with a tidal range of nineteen to twenty-six feet. At low water we were down in a canyon; at high water we were level with the trees on the shore. The sailing lives of the black-hulled Chilote boats were regulated by the tides. On every flood tide we saw a sail or two or three coming northward. On the ebb a few boats dropped down from Angelmó and headed southward and home.

The windward ability of the local sailing vessels was poor, but with a fair breeze and a favorable tidal stream they raced along at eight or nine knots over the ground. In calms an oar or two appeared. If a Chilote vessel seemed to be making much progress to windward you could be sure that an oar was working on the side of the vessel away from you.

The helmsman of a local sailing sloop generally bent his course a little when he spied the hull and mast of *Whisper*. The passing vessel would come close alongside so the crew could look us over. The people on board always seemed to be having a good time, almost as if they could hardly believe their good fortune at having a free ride on the wind and water. The nautical traffic went on in rain or sun, during the day and at night.

From my journal:

January 30, 2200 The air is warm and sultry and the stars are lovely and clear. Margaret and I were sitting talking in the cockpit earlier tonight when we heard a rustle of fabric. We looked up and there was a lancha Chilote a vela only a few feet away with her big gaff mainsail silhouetted against the dark sky that was brightened a little by a new moon. There were no lights on board and the black hull glided slowly along, the helmsman's cigarette a dot of red in the black.

The sailing vessel skimmed along slowly when suddenly the main halyards were let go and the canvas flapped to the deck in loose folds, the blocks squeaking as the halyards flew up. Someone tossed over an anchor and as the vessel swung away from the moonlighted sky, she disappeared in the night.

Puerto
Montt

Seno Reloncaví

Estero
Reloncaví

Isla
Guar

Cordillera

Isla
Puluqui

Isla
Abtao

Isla
Queullin

Isla
Tabon

42°S

Golfo

de

Isla
Caucahue

Isla
Llancahue

Estero Quintupeu

Buta
Chaques

Isla
Mechuque

Estero
Cahuelmó

Ancud

Isla
Tac

Estero Renihue

42°30'S

Isla
Caquache

73°W

72°30'W

SFM

FOUR

The Fjord in the Mountains

*W*E SAILED southward from Puerto Montt on a sleepy January morning bound for a place deep in the heart of the Andes. A sail in the mountains was something new to us and I fretted about the probable lack of wind. As we glided along in *Whisper* I marveled at the bluish scenery. Everything was part of a rainbow of blues—the mountains, the forests, the sky, the water, even a series of warm and gentle rain showers that looked like blue teardrops as they moved with the wind. In pouring rain we could only see to the end of the yacht. Ten minutes later the rain would drift away and the massive bulk of the *Cordillera de los Andes* was suddenly revealed with super clarity: a broad ribbon of cliffs and headlands and steep forests that climbed away to dazzling flashes of snow on distant summits.

Our destination was a place called Cahuelmó, about fifty-five miles to the south-southeast. By the late afternoon

(Overleaf) One day while anchored in Cahuelmó we had a visitor from another fjord who sailed over in his eight-foot dinghy, which used a slim branch for a mast, a couple of willow cuttings for a boom and sprit, a scrap of cotton cloth for a sail, and an oar for a rudder.

We became friends with Don Pedro, here seen with two of his sons on a calm day in this elegant fjord.

we had crossed Seno Reloncaví and part of Golfo de Ancud, two large inland gulfs. All day long we saw black-hulled gaff sloops piled high with sacks of potatoes and wheat going northward. Sometimes we had six or seven sails in sight at one time. We were in another century, in another world, with never the sound of an airplane or an automobile and only rarely the slow thump-thump of a fishboat engine or an inter-island ferry.

A friend named Jorge Piñeiro had suggested that we visit Cahuelmó. "It's an idyllic place and has wonderful natural hot springs," he said. "A half-hour soak will take ten years' wear and tear from your bones." Jorge clapped his hands together with pleasure as he spoke. "It makes me feel younger just to think about those marvelous soaks and all

that mountain grandeur. You'll be entirely by yourselves because the only resident is a man named Don Pedro who is a friend to all visitors as long as they don't steal his cattle."

"The Chilean *Pilot* says that winds of the fourth quarter —westerlies—blow in this estero with great violence," I said.

"Nonsense," said Jorge, who had been a Chilean naval officer and was now the master of *El Trauco*, a large Chilean yacht. "I have personally visited the fjord many times and have always seen it calm and peaceful during our summer trips. You *must* go."

When Margaret and I sailed in to Cahuelmó we saw that it was about one mile wide and three miles long, with a narrow entrance, forested walls that rose steeply from the water, and a cascading waterfall some 230 feet high that plunged noisily into the northeast corner of the bay. Most of the fjord was about 130 feet deep so we followed the local advice and dropped an anchor near the waterfall and ran a stern line ashore.

We were soon entranced by the utter tranquility of the place. We met Don Pedro and his four children. He was a cheery, quiet man who was raising his children single-handed because his wife had been drowned in a boating accident. Unfortunately, she—like many people close to the sea—could not swim. Don Pedro had formerly lived in Ancud but his home was destroyed in the earthquake of 1960. He had moved to Cahuelmó, built a house, and in addition to a few scratch crops and some chickens he ran a few cattle. He eked out his income by selling shellfish and smoked fish. He took his wares to Calbuco in the usual Chilote sailing sloop because there were no roads within fifty miles. The children went to school in the next inlet north, but it was too far to sail or row each day so the youngsters boarded with friends until the weekends when Don Pedro brought them home.

Cahuelmó seemed such a remote place for this man and his children. We gave them our old clothes and they brought us fish and beef. More important, Don Pedro rowed over for a little visit each day. It was fun to blow gently on the spark of our new friendship. I would pour a glass of wine and hand it to Don Pedro who would drink it down and hand back the glass with a shy smile.

At Don Pedro's suggestion we piled into the dinghy and rowed up to the steaming thermal springs which were so hot that you could scarcely touch the water. The local people, however, had led several cold rivulets of water to the hot springs, and by partially damming up the hot with a handful of moss and letting in some cold you could adjust the temperature. In addition the locals had hollowed out several bathtub-sized depressions in the soft volcanic rock. It was marvelous to have a hot soak under the warm summer sky with trees and ferns and wildflowers around you. If you

turned your head a little you could see mountains topped
with snow.

Sometimes in Cahuelmó we saw a pulling boat twenty or
twenty-five feet long come in for a load of shellfish. The two-
man crew worked in a strange fashion. One man put on a
headpiece breathing apparatus and plunged over the side

with a collecting bag. The diver's partner on board cranked a large handwheel connected to a small compressor that pumped air to the diver via a long hose. The men took turns diving and pumping. It seemed eerie, somehow, for a man to be below the surface of the sea with air pumped to him by his buddy above in the real world. There wasn't a sound connected with this lonely fishing. The only sign of the man below was the unending motion of the fisherman above slowly cranking the big iron wheel. It was spooky.

Cahuelmó was a good place to do a few small jobs on *Whisper,* to write some letters, and to study the next batch of charts that led toward Cape Horn.

Early one morning I suddenly awoke and felt the yacht pitching and rolling. I looked out and was horrified. The calm fjord was whipped by a westerly wind, the wind that supposedly never blew in the summer. We were trapped at the east end of the fjord near the shore and had to leave immediately. I cursed myself for ignoring the warning in the *Pilot* and for not having cleared out the evening before when the barometer had begun to drop and low clouds had blocked out the stars. Fortunately we had hanked on a small jib and had reefed the mainsail. I jumped into the dinghy and pulled myself along the stern line toward the cliff where the line was tied to a tree. As soon as I was afloat in the dinghy I realized why we weren't feeling well. *Whisper* was rolling all over the place in a wicked chop caused by the wind against the strong ebb that was pouring out of the fjord. The short waves slopped into the dinghy which was soon half full of water. I got as close as I could to the end of the warp and reached up with a knife, cut the line, held to the end, and signaled Margaret who quickly pulled the dinghy and me back to the yacht. We hoisted the dinghy on board and lashed it down.

Now we had the problem of beating out of the fjord against a headwind that was increasing by the minute. We ran up the mainsail and backed a small jib to get moving. I bent over the anchor windlass while Margaret tacked back and forth. The difficulty was that the strong wind wasn't steady but thundered down on us in irregular squalls from slightly different directions. The sails flapped frightfully when the wind headed us. After some effort I got up the chain and anchor and we began to beat toward the entrance.

If the wind had been a constant thirty or forty knots we could have thrashed our way out. But the wind was first twenty knots and then forty or fifty knots as the squalls shrieked down from the mountain heights. The wind heeled us over until the sides of the coachroof were in the water. Then all of a sudden the punch of the wind would be gone and we would be sailing along quietly. In the distance, however, I could hear another squall coming. With all the violent movement the engine wasn't much help because the propeller was out of the water half the time. (Over the years we have found that in really hard going the engine is relatively useless.)

The clouds began to lower and the wind increased in force until it threatened to blow me off the foredeck. The gusts buffeted me as if someone were punching my shoulder. I realized that it was hopeless to try to get out of the fjord because the squalls were rocketing down from the entrance every couple of minutes. The fjord itself had no shelter except at the upper end which was encumbered with unknown sand banks and shoals that dried out at low water, certainly not a place to explore with such winds behind us.

The only hope was to anchor out in the middle of the fjord. The holding ground was excellent white sand, but the depth was 130 feet which meant that we needed some 650 feet of cable. I dragged an anchor and two long warps to the foredeck, tied the lines together with a carrick bend, and began to fake down the lines. But as fast as I got a pile of line in order, a squall heeled the yacht and half the line skidded over the side. There was nothing to do but to start over. Again and again the line got tangled. There was some unintelligible shouting from the cockpit and gesturing about rocks but I waved Margaret onto the other tack. I went on sorting out the foredeck knitting like a seamstress gone wild.

The wind force escalated and the squalls whipped the water to a white froth. I had never seen such violence from wind and water in a restricted place. All land disappeared, the ship vanished, sight itself was blocked, and my eyes felt only the piercing sting of hail from the squalls. It probably sounds stupid, but the violence of the weather was beautiful in a way. I know that sometimes one's senses seem suspended, and an eternity of impressions flashes before the camera of the mind. For a second I seemed to look into the heart of the storm and to feel a strange kinship with the winds that were trying to destroy my little world.

Down at my feet the line tangles were hopeless because the deck was a teeter-totter that fell first one way and then the other. I looked around and saw that by some clever sailing in the lulls, Margaret had been able to get within a mile of the fjord entrance so we had a little sea room behind us. I motioned to Margaret to ease the mainsheet and then to come forward and hand the jib. Meanwhile I let out a forty-five-pound CQR anchor and all 210 feet of chain. The scope was less than two to one, but I figured the drag of the anchor would slow us down and hold the vessel somewhat until we got the line sorted out. With the yacht no longer heeling so violently, and with four sets of fingers frantically untying the tangles, we quickly sorted out the warp and let go a twenty-pound Danforth anchor and eased out 560 feet of line—a very long string. Both anchors held. We dropped the madly flapping mainsail and took careful bearings of landmarks. Even in the squalls we didn't drag. We were safe.

Around the perimeter of the fjord a dozen new waterfalls poured down from the heavy rain. During a clearing in the storm Margaret suddenly noticed a group of small figures huddled together on shore. Don Pedro and his children had watched our whole little drama.

We measured the wind when it eased a little. During the shrieking gusts, the indicator on the Swedish Ventimeter immediately shot to the top of the scale which meant sixty-three knots. Two days later this turbulent wind still blew and it wasn't until the third day that the noisy storm passed over and we were able to leave the fjord. The experience at Cahuelmó was a bit sobering. We were still twelve hundred miles from Cape Horn and already we had been severely flattened. Now when we sailed, one part of my brain would be tuned in to the nearest protected anchorage. No more open fjords for us.

Canal

Chacao

Golfo de Ancu

CHILOÉ

42°S

I. Mechuque

I. Buta Chauques

I. Tac

Castro

I. Quinchao

I. Achao

I. Antihue

Nercon

I. Apiao

I. Lemuy

I. Chaulinec

ISLA

Punta Queilen

I. Tranqui

43°S

Quellón

Golfo Corcovado

I. Coldita

I. Cailin

I. Laitec

73° W

74° W

SFM

FIVE

Black Hulls and Shellfish

*W*E SAILED toward Isla Chiloé which lay fat and green on the western horizon. The date was February 13 and a sixteen-knot wind blew warm and steady from the southwest. Margaret was in a good mood and she sat in a corner of the cockpit while she chuckled over a book by James Thurber. We worked up to a small island named Buta Chauques and skimmed along the southeastern shore past a band of kelp that floated parallel to the land. Above us rose the brown cross of a small church on the cliffs of the rocky island. Two hours later—with the setting of the sun—we rounded Isla Añihué close to starboard and slipped into the quiet water south of Isla Mechuque. Under the mainsail alone we slowly sailed near a small village. We noticed a group of people watching us. No one took his eyes off *Whisper.*

We anchored off the village in the place suggested by the Chilean *Pilot,* but three pulling boats came out at once and told us that we were in the way of night traffic. We were conducted to the *puerto* around the corner where we were surrounded by land on all sides. By the time we had anchored for the second time we seemed to be major news.

A half dozen boats were now tied up alongside. One man wanted to sell us chickens ("only 2,000 escudos. Very plump"). While I was declining the offer of the chicken salesman I saw out of the corner of my eye that a fishing boat as big as *Whisper* was coming alongside. And a second! One tied up forward and the other began to maneuver toward us. It was too much. I untied the first fishing boat, pushed it away, and asked the crew to come the next day. I turned to see two *carabineros,* with boots and smart uniforms, climbing on board from a pulling boat. Two girls who had come with the policemen also wanted to inspect the yacht, as did the rest of the welcoming committee. By the time night fell and everyone had left we had shown *Whisper* to forty visitors. Chicken feathers were all over the cockpit.

Mechuque (meh-chu-key) was a small hamlet of some seventy or eighty gray and unpainted clapboard houses with peaked roofs that were built around several low hills near the shore. We had been invited to the house of Fermin Grandón the chief *carabinero,* so we called on him to present our papers. Fermin invited us in for a breakfast of fried clams. The *carabineros* were the national policemen of Chile and had a reputation for fairness and uncorruptibility. (Unlike elsewhere in South America we heard that if you offered a bribe to a Chilean *carabinero* you were liable to go to jail.) Instead of being a national secret police, however, with all the undertones of that phrase, the *carabineros* that we encountered were more like friendly patrolmen on a neighborhood beat. We often saw these men in remote places where they kept law and order and always appeared neat and well groomed.

We met Fermin's two children and had a look around his house, which seemed somewhat overfurnished and cluttered with souvenirs. His wife was busy cooking in the kitchen. Fermin had a wind-up phonograph and was keen to play stirring *carabinero* marching songs, which seemed a bit much at 0830.

We went for a walk to see the village with Fermin's sister and another girl. The church was closed because there was no priest just then. We saw several small stores which had the usual canned goods, dried beans, sugar, rice, cooking utensils, and a few rolls of cloth. The island had too much rainfall for wheat and barley so the various cereal crops were often cut while green and taken into the kitchens of the homes and placed near the warm cooking hearths to ripen. Most of the men worked as woodcutters or fishermen and the village reflected these modest endeavors. We saw a few fishing boats up on the beaches, and one man was building a new cabin on an old hull. All the drinking water in Mechuque was fetched by hand from several wells and the people lighted their homes with kerosene lamps. There was daily mail service from Chiloé. The people had a simple life, but it seemed wholesome and pleasant.

We visited Fermin's house before we left and once again plates of delicious seafood appeared, accompanied by stirring *carabinero* marching songs on the phonograph. Fermin was delighted with our visit and presented us with a bottle of hard cider. He was a dear fellow but he was obviously miscast as a policeman. He should have been the leader of a brass band.

When we sailed from Mechuque, three old men stood on the beach and watched us, absorbing every move that Margaret and I made with the anchor and lines and sails. The three old men stood entranced. I felt a little self-conscious as if I were doing something wrong, so when we began to pull away I turned and waved good-bye. No one moved. The three old men stood perfectly still, filming us with their eyes. I went back to my steering and the chart. Before we changed course at the end of the island I turned and looked back. The old men were still watching. No one had moved. *Whisper* must have represented a dream, an escape, a change, a curiosity, a novelty, a transitory link with the universe beyond. Never have I seen three men look with such penetrating intensity.

We sailed westward to Canal Dalcahue where we an-

chored off the eastern shore of Isla Chiloé. This big island measured about a hundred miles from north to south and was thirty miles from east to west. In the early nineteenth century when Chile rebelled against the Spanish crown, the Spanish governors fled to Chiloé and in despair offered the island to England. George Canning, England's foreign secretary, turned down the suggestion, and in 1826 the last of the Spanish royalists were driven from the island which was Spain's final foothold in Chile.[6]

At the end of the eighteenth century Chiloé had three formal religious districts and fifteen Franciscan missionaries. Perhaps it was from these ambitious men of God two centuries ago that Chiloé derived its tradition of churches. Margaret and I saw churches everywhere—on prominent peninsulas, on high hills, in villages, along waterways, even on tiny islets. The churches were small, but astonishingly numerous. The Chilean sailing charts of this region were dotted with Maltese crosses.[7]

Everywhere were churches. Ahead, behind, to the right, to the left . . .

To find our position we only had to take the compass bearings of three churches on three different islands or headlands and then draw the lines on the chart. On foggy days we tried to follow the lead of the local sailors who kept track of land by listening for the barking of dogs.

Chiloé had a population of 111,000 that was clustered on the sheltered north and east sides of the island. There were two cities, Ancud in the north, and Castro in the east. Castro, with a population of 22,000, was located up a protected inlet far from the sea. I had read that the city had been settled by a Spanish explorer in 1567. I had also read that Castro had been looted, burned, and had suffered various earthquakes, fires, and floods during its four centuries. I expected a venerable walled city with an ancient church, old colonial buildings, and men on horseback.

The first sight of Castro revealed a skyline with the twin spires of a graceful church. The skyline also revealed the large A-frame of a new tourist hotel. Instead of men on horseback I saw men in Volkswagens. Instead of the mellowing stone of large colonial buildings we saw hundreds of small modern structures, warehouses with tin roofs, a bus depot, the towers of a radio station, and a crowded open market along the waterfront.

We had come in on the flood tide with a half a dozen black-hulled Chilote sailing sloops that were laden with people and produce. These local vessels sailed directly to the beach near the market to dry out. We anchored in a depth of thirty-three feet and lay near the route of motor launches that went back and forth between Castro and a swimming beach several miles across the channel. Each of the big fifty-foot wooden launches took fifty or sixty people and was pushed by a single twenty-horsepower Swedish Archimedes outboard motor, a low-rpm powerhouse that we often saw in Peru and Chile. It was a remarkable demonstration of the useful application of power.

My sea boots had begun to disintegrate so I rowed ashore to hunt for patches. Shopping is slow business in remote corners of the world but it gives you a chance to meet the people. The key is patience. I walked down the sleepy main streets, and after half a dozen false leads I found a likely looking hardware store. Inside I interrupted a card game to ask the clerk—the chief player—whether he had patches for rubber boots. After the clerk finished his hand he put down his cards, disappeared into a back room, and brought out a small patch made in Germany.

"Perfect," I said. "Have you a larger one?"

The clerk went to the back of the store again and after a few minutes returned with a bigger patch. "Give me six large and six small," I said.

The clerk was astonished. "Your boots must have many holes."

"Like a sieve," I replied, holding the fingers of each hand at right angles to the other to get across the meaning. "What about cement?" The clerk stopped for a minute to take a few sips of tea, disappeared into the back, and after some time returned with a tiny tube of cement.

"More," I said. "Bring me a dozen." By this time the card game had been forgotten. All the players had collected at the counter where they took a keen interest in my leaky boots and the patches. I had to explain who I was and where I had come from. Distant place names were meaningless so I said that I had sailed from Valparaiso, which resulted in a lot of worried looks.

Finally the clerk returned from the back room for the fourth time and triumphantly displayed twelve tiny tubes of cement. "Do you own a shoe repair shop?" he said. We all had a good laugh. My purchases were carefully wrapped and tied, and after some lengthy calculations the bill was worked out.

"Enough for many years," said the clerk as he presented me with my package. "No more wet feet." With smiles on every side I paid my bill (500 escudos), shook hands with the clerk and all the card players, and left.

Margaret and I shopped for food at the outdoor market along the Castro waterfront. We bought big purple onions and fresh string beans only a few hours from the vine. We loaded our canvas shopping bags with crunchy apples, luscious green cucumbers, heavy bunches of fat carrots, and eggs that were still warm. It was hard to stave off the women selling dried fish (very smelly) and those who

(Overleaf) We watched the little sailing vessels come in along the waterfront of Castro. We saw the men unload bulky sacks of potatoes and chupones, heavy boxes of shellfish, and the omnipresent sheep or two. Life for some of these people approached the barter system, but they always retained a sense of dignity, independence, and cheerfulness.

97

hawked lottery tickets ("Today is your day"), but we readily bought *chupones* which were the fruit of a thorny upland plant and looked something like artichokes. Each *chupone* had several dozen protruding seed stalks. You pulled out a single stalk, crushed the white inner end with your teeth, and sucked on it for a delicious pineapple flavor. When the taste was exhausted you plucked out another stalk, and so on. Children loved *chupones* and people all over town were chewing the stalks. When Charles Darwin visited Castro in 1835 he also noted that the locals were sucking seed stems from *chupones*, "a pleasant sweet pulp, here much esteemed." [8]

There was a great deal of sampling and checking in the market. A man would ask for an apple, take a bite, shake his head, and go on to the next seller. A woman would take a few cereal grains and earnestly inspect and taste them before deciding. A fish was never bought until the gills were looked at to see if the fish was really fresh.

All of the produce was sold by an old Spanish dry measure called an *almud* which is equivalent to a peck or a little less. Each seller had a neatly made box—roughly eight inches on a side—that had been handed down from mother to daughter for generations. You bought an *almud* of plums or half an *almud* of peas.

Local boats often came to market with some of the women on board clutching lovely bouquets of flowers. I am a sucker for ladies with flowers, so we always had a fresh bunch on the saloon table while we were in Chiloé.

Many of the women in the market wore thick hand-woven woolen skirts with a fringe at the bottom. The patterns were large squares of orange or dark green or brown with contrasting lines at the edges. Margaret liked the heavy wool and bought a one-kilo ball to knit a sweater. Meanwhile I negotiated for a fresh mackerel for dinner.

We discovered that an ordinary glass bottle was a treasure that was carefully saved for refilling or to turn in for a full bottle. There was no chance of purchasing wine, mineral

water, ginger ale, or cooking oil unless you had bottles to surrender. To get around the container shortage the housewives of Chile practiced constant bottle larceny. Margaret managed to collect a dozen bottles only after the most involved purchases.

"Six bottles of ginger ale please."

"Do you have the bottles?"

"No. Sell me the bottles. I will pay extra."

"Completely out of the question, *señora*."

"Where can I get bottles?"

"At the distributor's warehouse."

"Where is that?"

"I can tell you the address, but I must inform you that the company only sells wholesale and will not sell to you."

"Sell me three bottles. I will . . . ah . . . bring them back tomorrow."

"Ha!"

While we were in the south we found that shopping for ordinary items used by the people who lived in the region was easy and direct. We could buy local food, simple clothes, basic hardware, kerosene, soap, and aspirin without too much trouble. Getting unusual items or services was much harder. Nonregional foods, flashlight batteries, complex hardware, typing paper, radio repairs, and visits to a dentist were often hopeless.

To mail a package of exposed camera film to the U.S. was an all-day job.

"What's in the package?"

"Tourist films."

"You will need a stamp from Customs."

This meant a trip across town. The Customs man was about to go fishing and looked at my package with suspicion. "But it's going *out* of the country, not in," I pleaded. He stamped it.

Back at the post office the clerk didn't like my package.

"You must have a hole in it for inspection in Santiago."

"But I already have a Customs stamp."

"You must have the hole."

The postage charge for a kilo was 5,000 escudos or eight dollars. The only stamps, however, were in fifty-escudo denominations. Where can you put a hundred stamps on a small package? After some trial and error I stapled a piece of paper to the package and glued the stamps in place. I registered the parcel of course, but *certificado* was run by a bewildered woman who had obviously never handled an overseas package before. After thirty minutes at her window (with an impatient, lengthening line behind me) I was ready to swear off photography forever.

By now we had been around Puerto Montt, the cordillera, and Chiloé Island long enough to soak up a few impressions. The Chilote people were part Indian and part Spanish, with sparkling brown eyes, tanned faces, and coarse jet-black hair. The men were short and wiry; the women tended to be short and dumpy (the slim, stylishly dressed *señoritas* of Chile lived elsewhere). The Chilote men often wore tams or knitted caps and heavy sweaters of thick wool. They were almost all confirmed chain-smokers and great talkers who delighted in standing around discussing the weather, the qualities of old girl friends, or the next trip to Calbuco or Chonchi. Meanwhile the women worked industriously—selling at the market, cultivating in the fields, carding wool, and looking after the numerous children (once I saw a young lady nursing a child while she sorted mussels in a sailing vessel). It was common to see men talking and smoking in a boat while the women rowed. The men were clearly in charge, but I suspect that on an operational level the Chilote society was run by women.

The style of life was rustic and pleasantly primitive. The people were open and sincere and you couldn't help but hold out your hand to them because they were so trusting and direct. Our Spanish was terrible, but the Chilotes made an effort to follow our blundering efforts and somehow we were understood (gestures and diagrams on paper helped).

(Left) The hull sections of these load-carrying Chilote workboats have sharply flaring topsides. The main driving power comes from the large canvas mainsail. Note the brailing line from the leech of the sail to the gaff boom. This line leads down the mast to a convenient position so the sail area can be reduced quickly in case of a squall.

(Above) These vessels have gaff sloop rigs with crude fittings and gear, but the sailplan works well in these waters. The main boom is supported by fixed topping lifts which chafe the sail badly when the mainsheet is eased. In most parts of the world, gaff rigs have adjustable topping lifts which can be eased to reduce chafe. When I suggested this scheme, my idea was met with horror. "My grandfather used fixed topping lifts and what he did is good enough for me. Besides, a little sail sewing gives the women something to do."

How the Chilotes liked little jokes! I was keen to go for a sail on a local sloop so one day I went off in the *San Pedro* from Huequi to the next port. Margaret followed in *Whisper*. The *piloto*, Bernardo Peredes, and the *propietario*, Marcelino Nuñez, doubled up with laughter and amazement when they saw Margaret hoisting *Whisper's* sails, trimming them expertly, and beginning to overtake the *San Pedro*. I made a motion to Bernardo and Marcelino that Margaret might beat their sloop (we were running downwind). First the two men looked worried, but when they realized that I was joking with them, their laughter and good spirits knew no bounds.

We learned that the Chilotes have a rich and varied folklore of traditional beliefs, superstitions, and legends that rival the ancient Greeks and Romans. *El Millalobo* is the king of the sea. *La Huenchur* is a mysterious medicine woman. *La Pincoya* is the golden-haired daughter of the seashore and beaches who controls the shellfish. Dozens of

(Left) The piloto, *Bernardo Peredes. (Right) The* propietario, *Marcelino Nuñez.*

While I sailed on the San Pedro *and watched Bernardo Peredes steer, Margaret sailed alongside. Here she is forward adjusting a line while* Whisper *looks after herself.*

intricate stories and characters tell about everything from the creation of the land to man's sicknesses and death. To explain the birth of a child, for example, the legend of *El Trauco* introduces a sort of demon spirit of love in the form of an ugly dwarf with hypnotic charm who goes around seducing young unmarried women who want to run away but can't . . .[9]

(Overleaf) The fishermen's village of Nercon was built on wooden piles along the shores of these lovely hills that climbed westward from the sea a little south of Castro. On the water people traveled by boat; on the land they walked or used donkeys.

107

At Nercon we saw this ship's carpenter planking up Chilote workboats.

We sailed to nearby Nercon, where there was a small shipyard, and walked among a collection of old fishing boats, a new launch under construction in a shed, and a twenty-six-foot double-ended sailing vessel being built outside. The work was rough and crude. Half a dozen frames were cracked and one of the planks was split, but the whole job from the order to launching was to take only fifteen days. The planks were fastened with copper nails which were bent over where they emerged from the frames. The men eyeballed most of the planking and worked quickly. The yard crew also sewed the sails. Previously the men had built a sailing workboat that was fifty-nine feet long and the year before had constructed a thirty-foot sailing yacht named *La Pincoya*.

As we traveled south we passed fishing villages whose dwellings were built on high pilings along the edge of the water. One morning we dipped our flag to a big government health vessel which traveled from island to island with a medical staff on board.

All transport moved by water and a man's boat was as important to him as an automobile is to an American. Often we had half a dozen sails in sight when we traveled. In calms, oars appeared. Until I went to Chile I never realized how effective oars could be. We saw people rowing everywhere. It was common to have several oarsmen, each pulling on an oar ten to thirteen feet long. When the wind dropped, we watched heavily-laden sailing craft moving steadily and smoothly with a couple of oars. Once I was in a heavy *lancha* sixteen feet long (with a dozen people and their baggage) that was pushed by oars and which made reasonable progress. The blades of the oars were narrow and the rowers generally pulled with a short jerky motion, not a long smooth sweep.

The blessing of southern Chile was the abundance of shellfish. No one ever went hungry. On a minus tide the people scurried along the wide shorelines as the water receded with gurgling and sucking sounds. The trees and banks seemed high above us as we floated on a lowered ocean.

The water was low—down twenty-six feet—and a whole new world of sloping shoreline lay exposed. The women were humped over, bent down after clams and other goodies, their finds dropped in baskets carried in their left hands. Men dug

with wooden rakes among the seaweed or with old shovels in the mud. Loudly yelling boys competed with one another to get something choice. Old men carried string bags and scratched with hoes. Dogs sniffed and barked and ran along the exposed shores. A thin man in high boots industriously raked up a special sort of seaweed and shoveled it into baskets which he dumped into his rowboat. Young children clutched toy containers and mimicked their elders.

Everything was hurry! hurry! because the extreme low water lasted less than an hour. Once the crops were covered, the chance was gone. You could easily tell the sex of the picker by his track. The women seemed more patient and their nimble fingers quickly turned over rocks while their bodies scarcely seemed to move. The men all used tools, dug violently, and left disturbed mounds behind them.

Other people worked in the shallows from small boats and employed long poles with wire nets on the end. A man in yellow oilskins reached as low as his tall pole could go and groped blindly for special small shells. A little way down the beach a cow munched uneasily on yellowish seaweed that had been exposed by the low water. Across the channel on a point of land in the distance I could see other human figures bent over plucking a harvest of shells.

I listened to the sounds of the digging: the rasping, scratching, scraping, the clunking of rocks, the squeal of

This church at Achao was said to be the oldest on Chiloé. We heard a date of 1832 mentioned, not far from the time of Darwin, Fitz Roy, and the Beagle. The architectural style is curious and includes arches, two types of windows, three kinds of shingles, and a square-sided tower surmounted by an eight-sided cupola. Obviously the structure is very old and has gone through many restorations, including the recent concrete piers for the columns that support the arches. Looking at the church made me feel that a carpenter from England or the northeastern U.S. must have had a hand in the design at some stage. Inside, the church was surprisingly large with an open plan, but the interior seemed damp, dark, and drafty.

shovels on stones, the slurping of a pole being withdrawn. I watched while the shellfish people furrowed and inspected, probed and fingered, and dug and sifted in the mud and sand along the edge of the vast inland Chilean sea. Now, however, the water began to rise. Suddenly the work was finished. The men and women stood up and stretched their stiff backs. The tools were wiped off; baskets were measured and combined. The women disappeared in the direction of their homes. The cattle climbed to the fields. The children ran elsewhere to play. The men sat on the high shoreline to talk and smoke.

We called at Achao to see a century-old church, and at Isla Apiao because I was intrigued by a U-shaped island whose interior was accessible to our draft at high water. In the sheltered inlet of Apiao we found a shipyard on a hill, a large oyster-farming operation, and we saw a marvelous woodcarving by a Chilote artist. We could have spent a month, a year, or a lifetime sailing around Chiloé which seemed endlessly intriguing. Many of the anchorages were beautiful. We had a date with Cape Horn, however, so we took advantage of fair northerly winds, sailed southward, and soon began to leave the neat checkerboards of cultivated fields behind us. The settlements became fewer and the familiar brown churches grew less common. No longer did someone immediately row out to see us and crash alongside when we anchored. I had often been cross at all the interruptions by the Chilotes. Sometimes I had complained bitterly to Margaret about the lack of peace and quiet. When we were no longer bothered, however, I confess that I missed the knocks on the hull and the questions from the alert and curious Chilotes. I suppose I was like the man who fussed about the noisy violin practice of his daughter but who missed the music when she was gone.

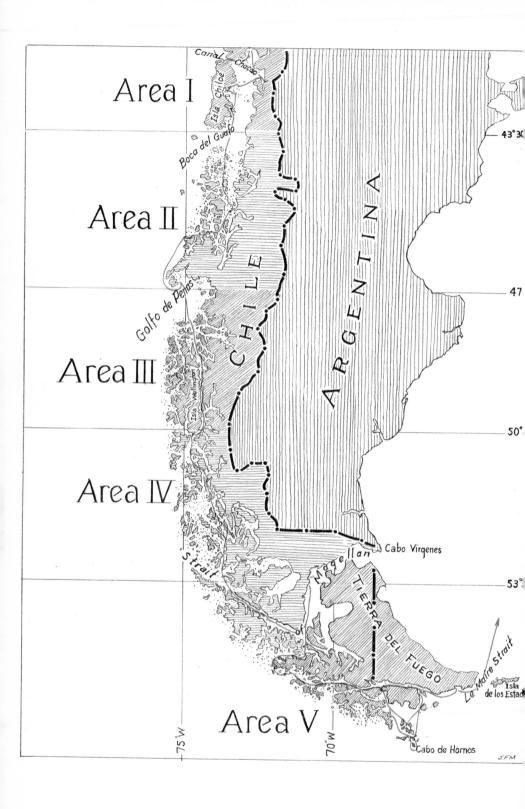

SIX

Who Was Anna Pink?

*F*OR PLANNING purposes I found it convenient to divide the Chilean trip into five parts. We had just sailed south from Isla Chiloé (Area I) and now were crossing the Boca del Guafo into the Chonos archipelago (Area II) which extended to about 47° S. Area III ran from Golfo de Penas to the fiftieth parallel of latitude at the south end of Isla Wellington. Area IV reached from 50° S to the Strait of Magellan and the city of Punta Arenas. Area V included the big island of Tierra del Fuego and Cape Horn.

Measured in a straight north–south direction, the distance lay between 42° and 56° S, which was fourteen degrees of latitude or 840 nautical miles. Our route was by no means direct, however, and when I totaled up all the bends, twists, backtracks, detours, false starts, and roundabout tracks of the whole trip, we found that we had logged 2,438 miles between Puerto Inglés in Canal Chacao and the west end of Isla de los Estados in Le Maire Strait.

Just now, however, we were entering Area II, the Chonos archipelago. We sailed across the Boca del Guafo in twenty-five-knot, gray, northwesterly weather. Astern, Isla Chiloé fell from sight. Four hours later we saw the first views of las Islas Guaitecas ahead to starboard. The islands rose up low and wooded at the base to somewhat barren and rounded heights of 1,200 feet. With this landfall we began a series of daylight runs from one isolated anchorage to another. Dense woods replaced the farming communities further north and the few fishermen that we saw were poorly dressed. The fishing sloops of the Chonos were small and crude, with high-peaked gaff mainsails of dark-brown fabric. Soon even those were behind us.

Margaret and I had four thick volumes of sailing directions or *Pilots* from the Chilean navy plus ninety-six nautical charts. In addition we had two volumes of British Admiralty *Pilots* and a few English charts to supplement the Chilean plans. We found the Chilean charts excellent and up-to-date. A small point was that land heights were sometimes poorly shown. I recall sailing alongside great cliffs in one place and looking at the chart which showed only blank white spaces —as if we were sailing on the Argentine pampas. The Chilean navy wanted mariners to stick to the main tracks so soundings were purposely omitted from side channels.

We liked the charts. The *Pilots* were also good and written in simple, direct Spanish so that even a couple of foreigners could work out the directions. The Chilean physical aids to navigation were poor, however, and some navigational lights were out or inoperative. Most beacons, markers, and monuments desperately needed repairs and painting. My guess was that the lights and maintenance had been neglected because of Chile's abysmal financial plight and because all transiting large vessels took Chilean pilots who had intimate knowledge of the waterways.

We found it regrettable that many of the beacons that marked channels and various critical places were not maintained. These monuments were all mentioned in the *Pilots* and drawn on the charts and obviously had been erected at great cost and effort by the navy in the past. In spite of this problem, however, the *Pilot* books and charts were quite adequate for daylight traverses of the channels.

Day after day we sailed southward along the various waterways—Perez Norte, Perez Sur, and Moraleda. We generally logged thirty to fifty miles on each run and found lots of good anchorages. It was early March and the prevailing winds blew from the north. With fair winds the

sailing was easy and pleasant. We seldom saw settlements or people.

One afternoon I had a nasty scare. A big rusty steel-hulled fishing boat steamed close to us. For a moment it reminded me of the vessel that had come alongside us off the Peruvian coast four months earlier and had demanded whiskey and cigarettes. When I demurred, the scowling Peruvian captain had threatened to ram the yacht and had sheered off only when I got out the Winchester thirty-thirty rifle and fired two shots into the air. But now as I looked across a bit nervously I saw only smiling faces on a Chilean navy workboat. We quickly ran up our U.S. flag and dipped it and watched a Chilean crewman hurry to lower and raise his trim red and white flag with a white star on a blue canton.

We stopped at a little village named Puerto Aguirre, near the entrance to Seno Aysén. The settlement was way out in the wilds and was a ragged little place that existed on fishing, and shellfish collecting and canning. Large or small, however, these remote hamlets always had two *carabineros*, a generating plant for electricity, radio communications, a proper schoolhouse, and an alert group of fishermen. When we changed course to sail up near the settlement, the wind came from ahead so we began to tack back and forth. All at once we noticed a group of people on shore watching our approach. As we sailed abeam of the men standing on the beach next to their open boats we began to get the unmistakable hand motions that indicated we should anchor. We sailed a little further, dropped the jib, anchored, and fell back to the suggested spot. Soon a dozen of the locals were on board to check us over.

Late that afternoon when everyone had gone, a leaky old rowboat pulled alongside. A pretty young woman sat in the sternsheets and held a baby on her lap. A rather disreputable-looking, unshaven man was rowing.

"Do you want to make a lot of money?" asked the woman.

"Why not?" I answered without risking anything.

"You must give me things to sell."

"What do you want?"

"Good clothing."

I made a motion to take off my trousers.

"Oh, no," she said with a marvelous laugh. "I mean extra clothing. New things."

While this conversation was going on I noticed that water was creeping up inside the rowboat. The woman moved her feet upward on the curved sides of the boat to stay ahead of the water. I motioned to the couple to climb on board *Whisper*. The woman shook her head. I offered a bucket to the man and made motions of bailing. He was clearly not interested.

"Do you have any French perfume?" asked the woman.

"French perfume?" I almost dropped the bucket. "What would you do with French perfume?"

"Sell it! There are many opportunities here." She gave me a sly glance and made vague motions toward the shore. I looked where she indicated but all I could see was a great pile of purple mussel shells and a dozen old whaleboats.

"Er . . . how much do you want?" I said.

"Bring me many large bottles of French perfume. I can sell them all. You will get much money—and perhaps more." She smiled up at me mischievously. "I must go now," she said. I swallowed nervously. Who was this charmer?

By this time the rowboat was one-quarter full of water. The woman continued to work her feet up along the sides of the hull to stay ahead of the water. Her child eyed the water fearfully and clutched at her mother's neck. The man at the oars had boots on and sat dumbly waiting until the woman nodded and he began to row.

I watched the boat go to the shore. The people climbed out, pulled the boat up on the beach, and trudged up the muddy track without looking back. What could this woman possibly do with French perfume? Sell it to the crews of passing vessels? But how many ships stopped in Puerto Aguirre in a year? How could I find the woman again? Would I want to? If the woman made money smuggling, she certainly didn't spend much on her water transport. Her boy friend didn't look any too prosperous either. In any case she was certainly an appealing smuggler, and if she had worn a few drops of the French perfume she could have unfrozen the cold heart of any passing captain.

That night the wind blew at thirty knots from the north but the holding ground was good and we were well anchored with plenty of chain out. Once when I got up to check our position I noticed that our kerosene anchor light had blown out. While I was relighting it I saw that a small coasting ship had anchored behind us. Maybe with a cargo of French perfume.

The next morning we watched the village while we got ready to leave. Wind-blown smoke raced downwind from

As we traveled south, the local vessels got smaller and cruder.

each house and the branches of the scrub trees rattled in the gusts. The fishermen worked at their boats drawn up on the beach and unloaded mackerel and sea bass. An old woman in a ragged brown sweater struggled to carry heavy firewood to her house. Children played nearby (no one offered to help the old woman). Higher up on the beach a new boat was under construction but there had been delays and its partial planking was gray with time. A man staggered along with a sack of flour and disappeared up the track into the woods. In the distance young girls skipped rope and their laughter rang across the water. Two women stood talking on the porch of a house while another woman shook out a blanket from an opposite upstairs window. Several boys took turns shinnying up the mast of a boat and then sliding down with shouts. Meanwhile the old woman in the ragged brown sweater struggled by herself with the firewood.

We sailed south along Canal Errazuriz and east by way of Canales Chacabuco and Pulluche. One night we stopped at Estero Balladares and anchored near a freshwater stream that ran into the protected bay. The water was smooth and quiet except for some commotion caused by a dozen ducks that beat the water frantically with their wings. At first I thought the birds were driving small fish before them into the shallows but later I found out that we had been introduced to loggerheads or steamer ducks which, unable to fly, beat the water to a froth in their frenzy to run away from danger. We got to know these strange birds well and often saw them madly flapping away when we entered isolated anchorages. According to my friend Bill Tilman, who had sailed these southern waters in his Bristol Channel pilot cutter *Mischief*, you had to be mighty hungry to relish a steamer duck.

Whether steamer duck should be called food is "a point verging perilously on the moot" [he wrote]. Our duck had been hung for three days, boiled twice, cooked in a pressure cooker, and served curried, yet still it had about it a pungent flavour of steamer duck —that is, of fish oil. Many years have passed since the Rev. Dr. Folliot justly observed that "the science of fish sauce is by no means brought to perfection—a fine field of discovery still lies open in that line"; yet in Patagonia the field has been neglected, as yet no sauce has been discovered that will disguise the fishiness of steamer duck.[10]

We had a good rest at Balladares and since we had a sparkling mountain stream next to us we filled the water tanks and did the laundry. Passing ships sometimes stopped for water at Balladares and a dozen signs with the name of a vessel and the date were nailed to a tree next to the stream.

We followed Canal Pulluche a little south and then west into Bahía Anna Pink where we began to feel the familiar swells of the Pacific. With dramatic high cliffs to the south on our left we edged along past four small islands and slipped into an anchorage.

Puerto Refugio lay on the edge of the Pacific and was surrounded by cliffs and mountains except for the entrance on the northwest side which was protected by half a dozen islets. While rain thundered down and low clouds swirled around the headlands we anchored off a beach on the southern side in sixty-five feet. When I had first seen the term *puerto* on a Chilean chart I thought that perhaps docks or ship facilities existed, but in truth *puerto* was merely a protected or partially protected place to anchor. The last three anchorages had been quite deserted and there didn't seem to be a soul within a hundred miles.

Puerto Refugio and Bahía Anna Pink dated from Commodore George Anson's voyage of 1741 against the Spanish. Anson's English fleet consisted of six fighting ships and two supply vessels, a 200-ton pink named *Industry* with twelve crew, and a 400-ton pink named *Anna* with fourteen crew (the term *pink* referred to a small three-masted bark with an especially narrow stern). The men of the expedition suffered terribly from scurvy during the long trip from England to the Pacific via Cape Horn.

(Overleaf) From our anchorage at Puerto Aguirre we looked at this scene of small houses, whaleboats, fishermen, and wood-gatherers.

While off the coast of Chile at about 46° S, the *Anna,* separated from the rest of the fleet, got involved with a westerly gale and was driven eastward toward the land. The captain—Master Gerrard—attempted to anchor near Isla Inchemo but squalls drove him toward the mainland and it seemed that the *Anna* would be wrecked for sure. At the last minute, however, the crew spied an opening in the cliffs ahead and steered into a well-protected bay. The ailing men lived in the refuge for two months and cured their scurvy by adding shellfish and wild vegetables to their diet before sailing onward. The anchorage was named Puerto Refugio and the larger area was called after the pink *Anna,* which in lubberly fashion has been corrupted to Bahía Anna Pink.[11]

Thirty miles to the south lay Rescue Point which was named by Fitz Roy aboard the *Beagle* on December 28, 1834:

While we were furling sails, some men were seen on a point of land near the ship, making signals to us in a very earnest manner. Being dressed as sailors, it was natural for us to conclude that they were some boat's crew left there to collect sealskins. A boat was sent to them, and directly she touched the land they rushed into her, without saying a word, as men would if pursued by a dreaded enemy; and not till they were afloat would they compose themselves enough to tell their story. They were North American sailors, who had deserted from the *Frances Henrietta* (a whaler of New Bedford), in October 1833. When off Cape Tres Montes, but out of sight of land, and in the middle of the night, these six men lowered a boat and left their ship, intending to coast along until they should arrive at Chiloé. Their first landing was effected on the 18th, but owing to negligence the boat was so badly stove that they could not repair her, and all their hopes of effecting a coasting voyage were thus crushed in the very outset.

Here in Estero Balladares, with unlimited fresh water from a mountain stream running into the anchorage, Margaret does some laundry.

(Overleaf) Looking across Bahía Anna Pink we see dark cliffs and hills that ring Puerto Refugio. It was here in 1741 that the pink Anna *found refuge.*

Finding it impossible to penetrate into the country, on account of its ruggedness, and thick forests, which, though only trifling in height, were almost impervious, they began a pilgrimage along-shore; but it was soon evident, to their dismay, that there were so many arms of the sea to pass round, and it was so difficult to walk, or rather climb, along the rocky shores, that they must abandon that idea also, and remain stationary. To this decision they were perhaps more inclined after the death of one of their number: who, in trying to cross a chasm between two cliffs, failed in his leap, fell, and was dashed to pieces. Their permanent abode was then taken up at the point which shelters Port San Estevan, now called Rescue Point; where they passed a year in anxious hope. Of course the few provisions which their boat had carried ashore were soon exhausted, and for thirteen months they had lived only upon seals' flesh, shell-fish, and wild celery; yet those five men, when received on board the *Beagle,* were in better condition, as to healthy fleshiness, colour, and actual health, than any five individuals belonging to our ship.[12]

From Bahía Anna Pink it was necessary to sail in the ocean for about one hundred forty miles because of a gap in the inland waterways. Part of this mileage was across the Golfo de Penas which had an evil reputation for storms, poor visibility, and unpredictable shore-setting currents. A weather forecast would have been helpful, but we had found it impossible to get such information in southern Chile. What broadcasts there were merely referred to conditions at the moment.

We waited until we had fair weather and a high and steady barometer and sailed from Puerto Refugio on a sunny clear morning with a fourteen-knot westerly wind blowing. We headed south and a little west to get an offing and by midnight we had logged sixty-three miles and were making good progress. At 0200 Margaret saw the flash of the Cape Raper light. I thought of the three watchkeepers at the remote lighthouse and the description written by Roz Davenport when the forty-six-foot Australian cutter *Waltzing Matilda* had visited the station in 1951:

The light was lit by paraffin. It had to be turned by hand, each man taking a watch through the night. It was beautifully kept, every single part polished and sparkling like a modern kitchen. I climbed inside the light itself while one of the men turned the handle—I felt like a white mouse in a cage, running on a toy wheel. Two hundred feet below, the Pacific crashed against the cliffs. Even at that height the noise of the wind and the seas was deafening and we could feel the building swaying with the force of the wind.[13]

At 0300 we changed from the genoa to a working jib when a series of light squalls dumped cold rain on us. At dawn I worked out a sextant sight from Venus to verify our position at the northern entrance to the Golfo de Penas. By 0800 we had double-reefed the mainsail and were running east-southeast with a thirty-five-knot wind on *Whisper*'s port quarter. The dark bulk of Peninsula Tres Montes was ahead to our left with Cabo Tres Montes somewhere in gray clouds in front of us. Because the wind was increasing I decided not to run for Canal Messier, which was fifty miles to the southeast across the Golfo de Penas on one of the worst lee shores in the world, but to sail instead to Puerto Barroso behind the shelter of Peninsula Tres Montes. It looked like an easy twenty miles. As we got close to the land, however, the fair wind that I had counted on gradually turned against us because it somehow worked behind the peninsula and mountains and headlands and now came charging toward us. Furious squalls began to dart out from the land, and the yacht heeled drunkenly as the wind hit the sails. By noon the wind was Force 8 from the north. Because of the weather shore there were no waves to speak of, but the sea was all white. Spray flew everywhere. Not only was the wind contrary, but we were obviously bucking some current or tidal stream—maybe both—and our progress was pathetic. It took us eleven hours to make good the last twenty miles to Puerto Barroso, no doubt our slowest twenty miles ever. When we finally anchored, we stripped off our soaking wet clothes and threw them on the cabin sole. Our faces were white from caked salt.

"I'm fed up," said Margaret. "How can you sail with such a sneaky wind? This Cape Horn route is paved with problems."

SEVEN

Condors and Shipwrecks

*S*LEET clattered on the deck and squalls whooshed over the bay every few minutes as we lay in Puerto Barroso waiting for an improvement in the weather before continuing south. The surprising thing about the place was that a squall would pass, the sun would come out, and the bay would be calm and quiet for a few minutes. But if I went on deck to do a small job, I would look up to find the sun suddenly gone and another squall roaring down on *Whisper*.

Quick! Grab the tools and get below.

The wind continued to blow hard from the north, switching abruptly to the south on the second day when the center of the weather system passed us moving eastward. Margaret and I watched streamers of storm-driven clouds run swiftly before the wind. Yet through breaks in the moving clouds we could see higher clouds that seemed almost stationary. The strong winds appeared to be below an altitude of a thousand or so feet.

The early nineteenth-century British survey ships had

In Puerto Charrua we sailed past this waterfall that was 432 feet high.

stopped near our anchorage in 1828 while charting these waters for the first time. Margaret and I had the distinct feeling that few people had been here since. We looked at untrodden sandy beaches and thick tangled forests of deep green that thinned out as the trees climbed the slopes.

On the third morning the sun shone brightly in the March sky and the needle on the barometer moved steadily to the right. While I recovered our anchors a condor circled overhead. The giant vulture had black plumage with white wing patches and a white neck ruff. Its flat lead-colored head was featherless and the neck had a wattle of loose skin. As the bird wheeled above the mast I could distinctly see light between the curved and separate dark feathers at the tips of the nine-foot wings and hear a rush of air with each flap. The bird was remarkable to see and made me think of dinosaurs and pterodactyls.

"Some bird," said Margaret. "Let's hope its appearance is a good omen."

We still had to cross the Golfo de Penas so we got out the chart and books to examine the fifty-mile gulf again. Normally the crossing of a small gulf was a trifling matter. Volume II of the Chilean *Pilot* suggested otherwise:

The gulf is particularly notable for the continuous and violent storms that sweep through the area, and for the large seas caused by the gales. A strong current from the west runs between Cabo Tres Montes and the entrance to Canal Messier. Great vigilance for navigation is advised during thick weather and in periods of poor visibility.

We started out with light winds which gradually freshened from the north. A few hours later we were running hard under shortened sail toward a frightful lee shore. We watched the fading summits of Tres Montes behind us and took bearings to check our east–west set, but low clouds and rain made it hard to see. We kept the mountains in sight for fifteen miles and then had only thirty-five miles to go, which should have been an easy dead-reckoning run. The problem, however, was how much to allow for the east-

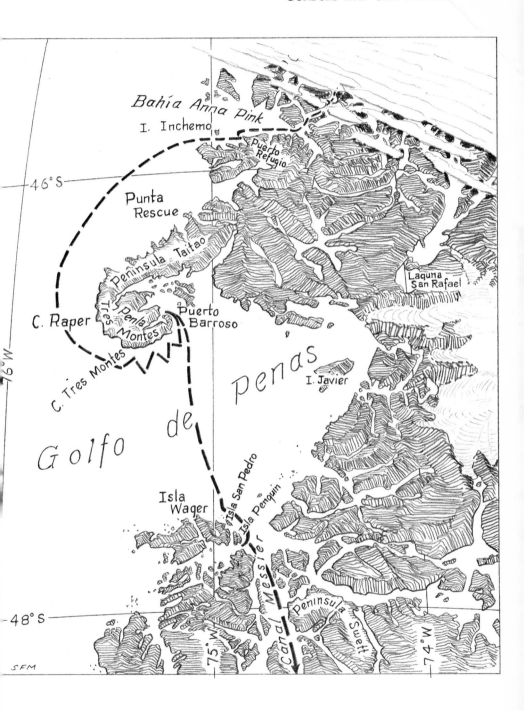

setting current. I figured fifteen degrees, but as the wind and seas increased, the steering was hard and our course was not exact.

I went below to tune our radio direction finder to the powerful San Pedro lighthouse radio beacon at the northern end of Canal Messier. I was quite astonished to find that San Pedro transmitted on 500 KC (Servicio QTG). My Brookes & Gatehouse RDF set stopped at 475 KC. In addition the station transmitted only on request which meant that with no transmitter on *Whisper* and an RDF set unable to receive the San Pedro signal there was no chance of radio assistance. Once again the RDF set was useless.

Because our east–west position was uncertain as we neared the southern shore of the Golfo de Penas I kept up enough sail to be able to push back into the thirty-knot wind if it became necessary to head northward into the gulf. Margaret steered while I stood forward with an arm around the mast and looked carefully ahead and to each side as I had done so many times before.

Sometimes a patch of dark cloud resembled a mountaintop. At other times I thought a breaking swell was a rock, but the only things I saw for sure were storm petrels and small black-browed albatrosses. Rain fell heavily. No wonder the trees and shrubs grew so thickly at this latitude. I said a silent prayer for all mariners running toward lee shores.

Suddenly I saw land ahead. We immediately turned eastward, hardened in the sheets, and began to see waves dashing against rocks and islets close to our right. We headed up a little to work offshore a bit and went along while I tried to fit an ill-defined shoreline into the sopping chart I held in my hand. All at once we saw the big steel towers of the San Pedro lighthouse. Marvelous! Now we knew exactly where we were. Margaret turned south-southeast and we left the land—Isla Wager—and the light station to starboard. An hour later we were seven miles south in Canal Messier, running nicely in smooth water, and about to round Isla Penguin into a good anchorage.

Isla Wager, the island we had just passed, got its name in

1741 when the twenty-eight-gun three-masted British ship *Wager* piled up on the north shore. Part of the same fleet that included the pink *Anna*, the *Wager* was one of Anson's ships bound against the Spanish. The beamy, bluff-bowed oak vessel had left England the year before, painted a proud yellow with a bold blue stripe around her upper works. Her cheering crew of a hundred sixty had hoped to become rich from plunder. But nine months later the ship was scarcely workable because of scandalous shipyard preparation, damage from heavy weather, and bad management. The officers and crew were miserable and only half alive because of scurvy. Thirty men were already dead; another hundred ten were to perish on Isla Wager and elsewhere; only twenty men got back to England.[14]

The next day the strong north wind continued. It was fair for us, however, and we were in sheltered waters so we hurried southward along Canal Messier. The north–south waterway was about three miles wide with small side branches here and there. The sailing was glorious. We had excellent charts, no navigational worries, and with only a headsail up we were able to surf along when a squall overtook us. High cliffs and mountains rose on both sides of this great natural canal. From time to time ravines filled with dark-green foliage ran back from the sides. Waterfalls poured down from unseen lakes and streams that had been charged to overflowing by the rain. Sometimes the storm clouds lowered to a few hundred feet and made a sort of wall between the sides of the channel. Masses of gray mist swirled and thickened and billowed while the rain and wind poured down.

A Swedish cargo ship passed us headed northward. I was glad that *Whisper* wasn't plowing into the seas and wind and wind-induced current that the big vessel seemed to take so easily.

When Margaret and I had sailed in Alaska we had learned that it is necessary to allow supplies and time for storm-bound days in port when you travel in such regions. No small vessel should try to make her way against great winds and seas unless such progress is very important, because such sailing is slow, uncomfortable, and hard on the yacht and the crew. The weather in many high latitude regions changes regularly, however, and if you wait a day or two or three you may get following winds and seas where before everything was against you. Often it is worthwhile to wait because you can make more mileage in one good day with fair weather than in three bad days with contrary winds.

We anchored in Caleta Connor after passing the Swedish cargo ship. That night the northerly storm blew itself out and gave us a week of light weather.

The next day while Margaret was steering she spotted another freighter. "There's a ship ahead," she called below. "Come up and hoist the flags so we can dip the ensign when we pass."

I ran up the Chilean courtesy flag and the U.S. flag. Something was wrong. Although the big ship was headed toward us our closing speed was slow; in fact the other vessel appeared to be dead in the water. It was only when we got close that we realized the ship was an abandoned wreck sitting on top of Bajo Cotopaxi, a mid-channel shoal. When we finally sailed past the blue, rust-streaked hulk we saw that she was the *Capitán Leonides*, an unfortunate Greek freighter.

Our route continued through Angostura Inglesa (English Narrows) about which the *Pilots* had pages of warnings and advice. We passed through at slack water with scarcely enough wind to fill the sails and wondered what all the fuss was about. In the northern part of the narrows lay Islote Clio, a tiny islet with a prominent white statue of the Virgin which had been erected by a well-wisher to give protection to passing mariners. At several places we saw the remains of Indian dwellings marked by enormous piles of purplish shells of clams and mussels. Granite domes and cliffs climbed high above the water, and snowfields glittered in the distance. When the weather was sunny it was a friendly and hospitable region and I was glad that we had come.

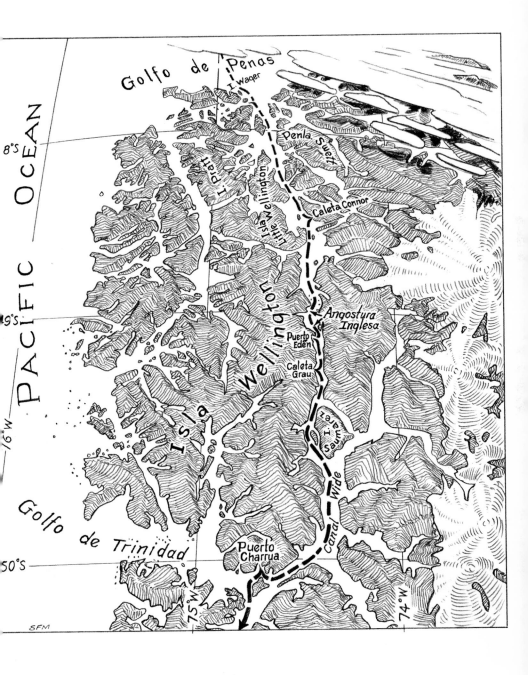

This vessel, the Capitán Leonides, *was a wreck jammed on top of a rock named Bajo Cotopaxi.*

We sailed into the little Indian settlement of Puerto Edén to have our clearance papers endorsed. We saw the usual uniformed *carabineros*, two good-natured souls who here took turns being the official welcomer, mayor, recorder, judge, dispenser of social welfare, crisis avoider, harbormaster, closer of the saloon, jailer, patient listener to one's woes, and in general a Father Superior. Like Indian settlements in most countries the two hundred or so Indians lived in a hodgepodge of tumble-down houses, but the village also had a dock, a school, and a post and telegraph office.

The next morning an Alacalufe rowed over to ask for used clothing. The man was one of twenty-three remaining pure-blooded Alacalufes, according to a *carabinero*. Our Indian visitor spoke softly but cleverly: "If you don't have any old clothes, new ones will do as well," he said. "I like blues and smart stripes." The man had a marvelous face, tanned and craggy, with large features and a mop of black hair.

Whether it was a face of resignation, suffering, cunning, or simply boredom I could not decide. We also got acquainted with an Alacalufe woodchopper who was incredibly skilled at shaping square timbers from *ciprés* logs with an ax.

A coasting ship anchored near us to unload a few supplies. I asked the radio operator whether he could unlock the secret of Chilean weather forecasts. He smiled, waved me inside his tiny wireless shack, flicked several switches, and suddenly—between bursts of nervous static—he was speaking to a confederate somewhere down the line.

"Hey, Luís, how is the weather?"

"The weather is very good today."

"Is it raining where you are? Look out the window and see."

At each port we stopped at in Chile we added an endorsement to our clearance which was soon almost six feet long.

"Just a minute. . . . Yes, it's raining hard."
"How's the wind?"
"Just a minute. . . . Yes, plenty of wind."
"What direction?"
"Just a minute. . . . Southwest, forty knots."
"The weather is very bad today."
"*Si*, the weather is very bad today."

Alacalufe Indian, Puerto Edén.

Our next destination was the Strait of Magellan, which took us seven more days of sailing. Each night our anchorage was increasingly dramatic as we voyaged closer to the heart of the high Andes. We crossed the fiftieth parallel of south latitude.

As we approached Canal Wide and skirted the high mass

of Isla Saumarez in a light rain I noticed a wisp of smoke ahead. Far out in the wilderness we came upon an Indian house where a man was splitting firewood. The figure looked up as we hove into view with our sails pulling hard. The chopping stopped in mid-stroke and the man turned to watch us, spellbound, as if we were an apparition of some sort. He didn't respond to my wave or shout but conintued to look at us as if we were a strange bird or a novel fish. Another man moved into the scene, also watching us. The two figures kept their attention on *Whisper* until we passed out of sight. A hundred, two hundred years ago, their forefathers might also have stared transfixed at earlier voyagers.

In Puerto Charrua we anchored near a 434-foot waterfall that roared into the water near us. I got in terrible trouble that night when I opened a portlight to let in a little air. I forgot that Margaret's bread was rising and that bread is temperamental stuff. The chilled loaves suddenly collapsed like punctured tires when the yeast stopped making CO_2. Margaret lost her temper. "No more bread ever," she cried. "I'm through. You'll have to make your own."

The next day we followed Canal Concepción and slipped into Puerto Molyneux where we anchored near two wrecks. The larger one was the *Ponderosa* of Monrovia, which was beached and in fair condition. Its cargo of rotting wheat smelled ghastly. The anchorage was a hundred feet deep so we put out five hundred feet of chain and nylon.

On March 22 we sailed through a wonderful mountainous narrows called Angostura Guia whose glacier-carved granite cliffs and canyons and ravines and domes reminded me of 10,000-foot mountain passes in California's Sierra Nevada. It seemed unbelievable to be sailing at sea level with such scenery around us. The northerly winds still held as we entered Canal Sarmiento and hurried south.

We stopped at Puerto Bueno which the Spanish explorer Pedro Sarmiento de Gamboa discovered and named in December 1579, some four hundred years ago. It seemed unreal to think of a sixteenth-century ship with a crew of fifty-four officers and men anchoring and mooring, taking on wood and water, collecting shellfish, drawing the seine, and climbing the local mountains to make the first crude charts of the region. As we looked around our comfortable yacht with her dry and rot-free fiberglass hull, Dacron sails, durable cordage, useful auxiliary engine, electric lights, winches, wire rigging, excellent charts, and healthy foodstuffs, we tried to imagine what sailing in these channels must have been like in 1579. Any sort of rational comparison was beyond us.

It is a mark of my ignorance that until I began to read the personal narratives of the early Spanish who explored the south and west coasts of South America I thought them all dolts who were almost always outwitted by the clever English. Such thinking is completely untrue and perhaps comes from my defective and oversimplified textbooks at school. Sarmiento, Cordova, Ladrillero, Hojea, and many others were talented and resourceful, as their accounts plainly show.[15]

We began to see large glaciers when we turned into Estrecho Collingwood. As we headed southeast the ice fields and glacier snouts on the northwest slopes of the mountains stood out bluish and enormous. The barometer was dropping again.

It was a bit upsetting to see the wrecks of so many large ships. We passed two more in Canal Smyth about twenty miles north of the Strait of Magellan. One big steel ship was on her starboard side with her propeller and rudder in the air. We read about two other wrecks near Boston Island and a third directly on our route. "If big ships get turned upside down, what chance do we have?" I said to Margaret.

We hove to at the Islotes Fairway lighthouse near the western entrance of the Strait of Magellan. I hoisted the flag signal UU ("I am bound for . . .") and then PA (Punta Arenas). We could see two uniformed lightkeepers watching us, one with binoculars and the second with a black volume, presumably the code book.

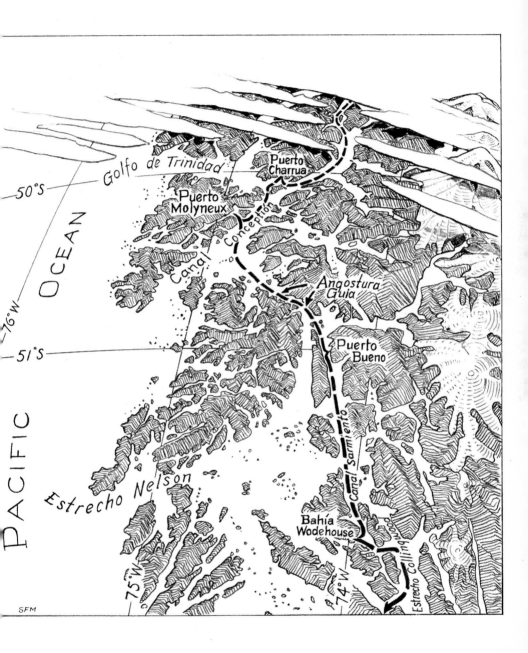

As we crossed into the Strait of Magellan and headed toward Isla Tamar the wind veered from the north to the west and began to blow hard. In the middle of the strait the waterway opened out and the scenery was awesome. I was keen to take a photograph of Cabo Pilar, the famous landmark at the southern side of the western entrance, but as I groped for a camera the historic cape disappeared in swirling mists of darkening rain and wind. Everything around us was gray—gray water, gray cliffs, gray mountains, and gray clouds. I could hardly believe that we had reached such a long-dreamed-of goal. It was wildly exciting, yet a bit unnerving.

Fifty miles to the northwest lay the Evangelistas lighthouse whose keepers put up with the worst weather anywhere. The lantern is 230 feet above sea level, yet during bad weather spray is flung on the glass. Taking supplies and a change of keepers to the light is a hard job for the Chilean navy. Once a relief ship waited for forty days to transfer men and desperately needed food. The ship stayed in the protection of islets southwest of Isla Pacheco about ten miles from the light while hoping for a respite from the westerly gales.

In the channels we navigated by constant reference to landmarks. Our main tools were the binoculars, the hand-bearing compass, and the charts.

(Overleaf) As we sailed south into Estrecho Collingwood we began to see bluish glaciers on the northwest slopes of the mountains bordering the Strait of Magellan.

Today these islets are called Grupo Cuarenta Dias (Forty Days Group).

I thought of the small ship sailors who had been here before and had gone westward from this place. It took Joshua Slocum (1896) seven attempts before he made a successful offing into the Pacific from the Strait of Magellan. Louis Bernicot (1937) made it on his first try. I shuddered to think of heading out into those Pacific graybeards.[16]

We spent an uneasy night behind Isla Tamar in Caleta Rachas (Squall Bay). The yacht did a ballet sequence all night and in the morning the two anchor cables were wound round and round each other. We cleared out promptly and were soon running eastward under a small working jib. We found the seas surprisingly large, caused by the gale pushing against the tidal stream from the east. The wind increased and we were soon surfing along. I knew that we were overpowered, but the sailing was so exhilarating and our progress so good that I hesitated to shorten sail.

From the log:

March 27, 1500 East of Cooper Key light. Whisper *broached to under the poled-out working jib. M. was steering and a wave shoved the stern to starboard. The sail got backed against the spinnaker pole. The wind pummeled down in furious gusts. (I was on the port side forward taking photographs.) M. got jammed against the starboard cockpit coaming by the tiller which was unmovable. We should have cut the jib sheet, but there was a lot of water flying around and some confusion. The eight-ounce sail blew out in a zillion pieces and we resumed course, making about three knots under bare pole. We consigned the remnants of the sail to the deep, a noble burial for an old friend.*

The anchorages were getting more chancy and the sailing was getting harder by the minute. No wonder we had seen so many big shipwrecks. Maybe the condor that had circled around us earlier was trying to tell us something. What lay ahead?

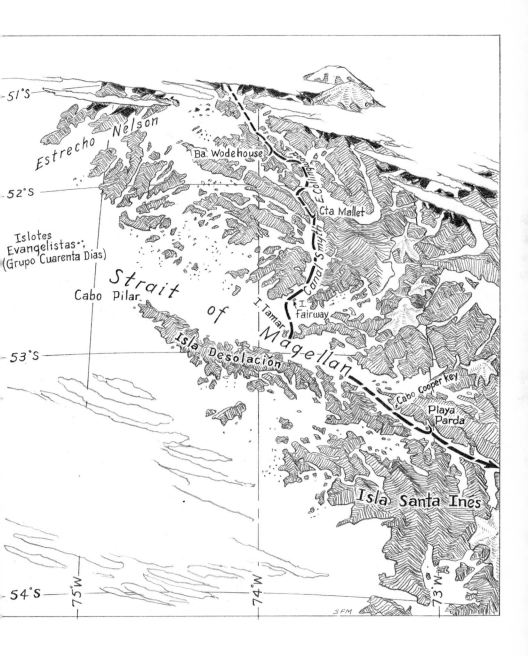

51°S

Estrecho Nelson

Ba. Wodehouse

Woodbury E. Co.

Cta Mallet

52°S

Islotes
Evangelistas
(Grupo Cuarenta Dias)

Cabo Pilar

Strait

Canal Smyth

I. Tamar

I. Fairway

of

Isla Desolación

Magellan

53°S

Cabo Cooper key

Playa
Parda

Isla Santa Inés

75°W

74°W

7.3°W

54°S

S F M

EIGHT

Strong Winds

SAILING in Cape Horn waters is like walking on a tightrope. As long as each of your steps is surefooted and in the right direction, all is perfection. In my view, small ship handling in the vicinity of the great Chilean mountains and glaciers is the most exciting sport in the world. Trouble lurks on all sides, however, and it takes only one slip to plunge into disaster.

The big problem is the wind, which can blow with violence that is hard for a distant reader to believe.

Cape Horn gales blow primarily from the west. As the depressions move eastward in the Southern Ocean at say 60° S, the wind to the northward blows first from the northwest, veers to the west, and finally blows hardest from the southwest. For more than one hundred twenty-five years, ship reports have verified that winds of at least Force 8 (34–40 knots) blow 23 percent of the time in the Cape Horn area. This means that you will find winds of thirty-seven knots and upward one day in four.

(Overleaf) Looking south across Bahía Playa Parda toward the Strait of Magellan which here runs east and west (to the left and right). There is a strong west wind blowing and you can see the wind-blown water streaming eastward in the distance. Whisper rocks from side to side as squalls strike the yacht. In the distance is Isla Desolación.

This is only part of the problem. Around mountains, the uneven heating and irregular topography introduce a turbulence factor of some 40 percent more and cause violent gustiness. Force 13 and 14 winds (72–89 knots) are no strangers to the Chilean channels, and Force 15 (90–99 knots) is more than casually known. A portion of the blame can be directed to the williwaw or Cape Horn squall:

The williwaw [according to the British *Pilot*], unlike most of the squalls which occur in tropical and temperate regions, depends largely, if not entirely, on the existence of strong winds or gales at sea at a height of several thousands of feet over the land. These strong winds generally prevail over an area of several thousand square miles. As they strike the rugged mountains of the archipelagos, they set up eddies of varying size and intensity. . . . During the strongest williwaws, which occur most often westward of Cabo Froward and near the main coastline adjoining the stormiest region at sea, the wind almost certainly exceeds 100 knots.[17]

For the fellow snug at home, such figures are mere numbers. Coming face to face with winds of these magnitudes in a small vessel, however, is an awesome test of man and boat.

Obviously no yacht or fishing boat or naval vessel or cargo ship goes sailing in hurricane winds by choice. You anchor in a sheltered place if possible and wait for better weather. In the channels there are many suitable bays, but ordinary anchoring techniques are quite useless when the wind begins to blow hard. In southern Chile all vessels— unless they are large enough to keep up steam and have crew to stand anchor watches—take lines ashore; otherwise they use radar and travel day and night.

Unfortunately, in the beginning you doubt the necessity of tying ashore. *My* anchors are better. *My* anchoring techniques are good enough. *My* judgement is adequate. Lines ashore? Mooring to trees? Humbug!

It is only after some months in the region, a careful reading of mariners' accounts, and discussions with other captains that you begin to get an idea of the scope of Cape Horn anchoring problems.

The strong winds blow from the west so you seek a bay or inlet that will protect you from westerly seas. Ideally, an anchorage should be on the east side of a long low finger of land that runs north and south or perhaps is a horseshoe open to the east. Low land to the west is preferred because the wind turbulence and resultant williwaws are less. Usually, however, a sheltered bay in the channels has mountains or steep hills on three sides. What you must do then is to try to predict where the westerly winds will funnel down, and to head the vessel in that direction. This means anchoring in front of a canyon or draw or low place in the hills that leads roughly westward. You sail up to such a place and creep as close to the shore as possible.

Sometimes a deep anchorage will allow you to go within a few feet of the shore; the water is often clear and you can watch the bottom come up. In addition the charts sometimes have detailed plans. Then you launch the dinghy and take lines to the land—generally two lines secured to separate strong points. If there are substantial trees or logs, you can tie to them. Otherwise you carry anchors ashore and dig them into the beach or earth, or jam the flukes in cracks in the rock if you're near a stony shore. The westerly winds will hold you off and it is easy to veer a little line and to drop a stern anchor to keep the yacht from swinging. Obviously anchor- and line-handling techniques are important as is a good rowing dinghy.

If all this sounds complicated, it is; but such a scheme is the only way of survival when the hurricane winds begin to blow. And exactly half the time the winds start at night which means that you are quite helpless in the pitch black because you can't see anything. Even during the day the visibility is often poor because of windblown spray. With a couple of lines to the shore and a little thought about protecting the rope from chafe, however, your vessel can withstand any strength of wind. The noise may be wearisome and the heeling from the gusts may upset your nerves a little, but you and your vessel will be safe.

I don't want to give the impression that the westerly gales are unremitting and that the sailing in the south is an endless nightmare of anchoring and storm sail handling. Sometimes the weather is beautiful with sunny skies and light winds for a week or two. Birds sing around the yacht. Seals play in the water. Laundry is on the line. All the portlights and hatches are open. The camera is out. A paint pot appears. You take delightful walks in the woods.

But one day the barometer begins to plunge. It is time to think about shelter and security. The sun vanishes. Heavy clouds race in from the west. The sky drops to mast-top level. The temperature falls. Rain and sleet begin to beat on the deck. The world becomes constricted and sullen and gray. Look out!

In the Strait of Magellan we were blown out of two anchorages in spite of substantial anchors, lots of scope, and good holding ground because I hadn't caught on to the idea of tying ashore at night or during violent storms, a concept I was to learn little by little. On March 30 we had anchored in Puerto Gallant, the inner part of Fortescue Bay.

My journal noted:

I happened to look out and noticed that we were very close to Wigwam Island, the islet that divides Fortescue from Gallant. The island had a lot of bushes of the most marvelous shades of light green. I was fascinated by the colors and how the bushes were moving in the wind. Wait a minute! The bushes weren't moving. It was the yacht! Yikes! We were dragging merrily down the bay. I had the sense to pull on my oilskins before I went on deck and it was fortunate that I did because I was out in hurricane force winds for the next three hours.

We picked up the anchor and put it down four more times, each effort in a different part of the bay. But on every attempt the CQR dragged home hopelessly fouled with seaweed and kelp. We dropped a 33-pound Danforth only to have it also come to the ship with a huge tangle of kelp. By now it was almost dark so we hurried outside into Fortescue

Bay where the water was deeper. I dropped the CQR and we held on all night, a rolly and miserable time. I had strained my back and the yacht was a mess from the seaweed and lines and anchors. Fortunately there was a small navigational light at Fortescue which gave us a handy point to take anchor bearings at hourly intervals.

I wasn't alone in my trouble at Puerto Gallant. In January 1768, more than two hundred years earlier, Louis de Bougainville had written: "A dreadful hurricane came suddenly from S.S.W. and blew with such fury as to astonish the oldest seamen. Both our ships had their anchors come home, and were obliged to let go their sheet-anchor, lower the lower yards, and hand the top-masts: our mizen was carried away in the brails." [18]

The next day we rounded Cabo Froward, an impressive, heavy-browed mountain that climbed to 1,178 feet immediately above us. This point marked the southernmost extremity of the mainland of South America. To the south lay Tierra del Fuego and a scattering of small islands, one of which was Cape Horn. Here the Strait of Magellan turned northward.

It was exciting to sail in such famous waters. Thoughts of Magellan and his chronicler Pigafetta flashed through my mind. It was past this place that Francis Drake sailed in August 1578 with his fleet of five vessels. Drake soon learned about the williwaws: "Two or three of these winds would com togeather & meet . . . in one body whose forces . . . did so violently fall into the sea whirleing, or as the Spanyard sayth with a Tornado, that they would peirse into the verry bowells of the sea & make it swell upwards on every syde."

(Overleaf) The southern tip of the continental mass of South America is Cabo Froward, here seen rising above the Strait of Magellan. For many years an enormous iron cross stood at the top of Cabo Froward, but the monument was blown away in a fierce storm. A second, reinforced cross was raised, this time to stand forever. Unfortunately, the wind was stronger than the iron, and the second cross blew down.

Drake made the 334 nautical miles of the Strait of Magellan in only sixteen days (Magellan took thirty-seven). He then went on to terrorize and ransack the Spanish towns and shipping on the west coast of South America and eventually sailed west-about to England with the *Golden Hind* almost sinking from the weight of silver and gold booty.[19]

The Spanish viceroy of Peru sent Sarmiento to the Strait of Magellan to fortify the place against future incursions by the infamous Francisco Draquez, as he was called. Sarmiento thoroughly inspected the strait and then sailed to Spain where he recommended to Phillip II that the strait be fortified and colonized. A great fleet of twenty-five ships and some thirty-five hundred soldiers, clerks, and colonists (including women) left Spain in September 1581. From the beginning the fleet had grievous problems. Many of the vessels were rotten and foundered in severe weather, and by the time the ships had crossed to Brazil the ragtag squadron was sorely depleted by desertions, drownings, disease, and continuing thievery. Some of the leaders went elsewhere, the fleet started, turned back, and restarted. Sarmiento finally reached the Strait of Magellan with only five ships, thirty months after leaving Spain.

In February 1584 Sarmiento landed three hundred people near the eastern entrance and founded a settlement called Nombre de Jesus. One of his vessels was wrecked while unloading stores. Three other ships deserted and fled. Sarmiento took a hundred soldiers and traveled overland and set up a second village Rey Don Felipe, at Puerto Hambre, a few miles north of Cabo Froward. But bad management, marauding Indians, and squabbling doomed both settlements from the start.

This alert creature is a guanaco, closely related to the llama, alpaca, and vicuña. The extinct Indians of the Ona tribe on the eastern end of Tierra del Fuego hunted and lived almost exclusively on this animal. Note the open, flat, rolling land toward the eastern side of the Strait of Magellan, an abrupt change from the mountains further west.

Sarmiento sailed off in the *Maria*, the last ship, to get supplies in Brazil. He loaded new stores and tried to get back, but gales drove him away. He finally decided to return to Spain to organize a genuine relief expedition. On the way, however, he was captured first by the English and then by the French and held prisoner for three years. It was the end of 1589 before he got back to Spain where no one had any interest in the poor colonists at the other end of the world.

When Thomas Cavendish sailed to the strait in 1587, on a voyage in which he tried to emulate Drake, he found only a handful of starving Spaniards. Sarmiento's great scheme had failed miserably. The whole story of Sarmiento reads like a fanciful romance and could be the vehicle for an opera if the actual happenings weren't so tragic.[20]

As we looked at Cabo Froward and the dark waters of the strait, I could almost see the *Beagle* battling westward on her first survey voyage in 1827. I reflected on Theodore Roosevelt's great white fleet of U.S. battleships that had steamed westward from this point in 1908. The Chilean cruiser *Chacabuco* proudly led the sixteen enormous coal-burning capital ships at ten knots as they kept an interval of four hundred yards between ships while hoists of brightly colored code flags fluttered from the signal yards.[21]

I thought of 1914 and the Battle of Coronel and how the doomed British fleet had steamed past this spot on its way to meet the Germans. And finally I remembered the plucky yachtsmen—Willy de Roos of Belgium and Tom Zydler of Poland—who together with their crews had sailed past this place only a few months before us. I said a quiet prayer for all these adventurous men, their countries, and their varied reasons for coming.[22]

That afternoon we anchored in Bahía Bougainville, a snug cove about one cable wide, "completely sheltered from all winds," according to the *Pilot*. In an impressive calm we anchored in forty-two feet—in good holding ground of mud and shells—and with two hundred ten feet of chain out we were unable to drag the yacht toward the mouth of the bay even by jerking the yacht with the full reverse power of the engine. We turned in early and hoped for a good rest, but in the dim hours of the night the wind started to howl. I routinely got up to shine a flashlight at the trees, only to have my hair stand on end when I saw that we had been blown out of the bay—chain and all—and had almost dragged up on a small island to the east.

Sleep was finished. We put up storm sails, recovered our anchor, and sailed forty-three miles northward to Punta Arenas. The wind was forty knots from the west-southwest and the strait was a mass of white water, but we sailed about a half mile off the weather shore where in only eighteen-inch waves we made good time, although we heeled plenty in the squalls.

This business of getting blown out of anchorages was no rarity. Joshua Slocum's *Spray* was repeatedly flung out of anchorages while sailing in the Strait of Magellan area. In March 1896, Slocum wrote: "While I was wondering why no trees grew on the slope abreast of the anchorage, half-minded to lay by the sail-making and land with my gun for some game and to inspect a white boulder on the beach, near the brook, a williwaw came down with such terrific force as to carry the *Spray*, with two anchors down, like a feather out of the cove and away into deep water. No wonder trees did not grow on the side of that hill! Great Boreas! a tree would need to be all roots to hold on against such a furious wind." [23]

The British *Pilot* mentioned tree damage with alarming regularity: ". . . squalls are probably frequent, and must blow with great violence, for there are trees torn up by the roots." [24]

The mountainous geography of the Andes changed abruptly as we moved northward toward the eastern entrance of the Strait of Magellan. The land became low and flat and drier. Trees vanished. The few hills were golden with dried grass and you could see long distances across the land. We

The port of Punta Arenas is a poor place for large and small ships because the Strait of Magellan is eighteen miles wide at this point and there is no protection from the sea. The vessels shown here are on the lee side of the dock while a westerly wind holds them off. A wind shift, however, means that all the vessels must move to the other side of the pier.

began to notice a few ranches and buildings.

Punta Arenas is the principal Chilean city of the south, and is on the western side of the Strait of Magellan at a point where it is eighteen miles wide. The city has a population of 65,000 and, in addition to being the navy headquarters for the region, handles a good deal of wool and mutton. There is a shipyard, airport, some light manufacturing, and the city is a shipping center for oil, gas, and coal, besides handling coastal traffic. Unfortunately there is no proper port,

only a long dock that extends southward. In westerly winds everyone ties to the eastern side of the dock or anchors out. A good deal of the beach area is littered with wrecks of big and little vessels, and accounts of drownings from people going ashore from ships anchored in the open roadstead are dotted all through travelers' accounts.[25]

While we were there a violent local storm called a *panteonero* (a cemetery wind) blew up and brought Force 13 winds (72–80 knots). During the big wind I retreated below and read about early flying in the area:

The French pioneer airman Saint-Exupéry wrote some vivid descriptions of the effects of the cyclones and whirlwinds in southern Argentina, "the country of flying stones," as he called it, because large stones were literally flung into the air and hurled about by the howling wind. On one occasion, after landing his plane with much difficulty he had to fight for hours against the diabolical strength of the hurricane, which was rolling cattle over and whipping roofs off houses. He asked for assistance from local troops, and with hundreds of men lying on the plane's fuselage and others clinging to the undercarriage, holding the plane down, he was able at last to run it into the hangar.

Again, when Saint-Exupéry was pioneering the air-route down South America to the Magellan Straits, for the French postal authorities, strong winds over Patagonia forced him to land when 200 miles from Punta Arenas. He took off again the following day, being airborne in a matter of yards—literally plucked from the ground by the headwind. But an hour later he could still see the landing strip he had taken off from; and after six hours' flying against the wind he had covered no more than 160 miles, although the plane had a 400-h.p. engine.[26]

I looked out from inside *Whisper* and saw that the Strait of Magellan was a mass of foam. The fear among the massed small boats on the lee side of the dock was that the big German cargo cranes would topple over and fall on the vessels. The navy officers all had the visor straps of their hats down under their chins to keep their hats from blowing away. People moved on the dock like cats, mostly on all fours, and went from handhold to handhold. But two days later the storm was suddenly over, and life on the dock was back to normal. Small boys bicycled up and down while stevedores moved crates of onions.

Some years ago Margaret and I made a long trip in the Pacific during which we produced a 16-mm documentary film. We lectured with the film in order to raise funds to continue our travels. Now we were attempting to make a new film about our Cape Horn trip. But the trouble with film work on a small yacht is that when the action is best you are quite busy dealing with various problems and have no time to shoot film. In the Chilean channels there was so much to do that a forty-eight-hour day wouldn't have been long enough. So I hired an American photographer to join us for the sail from Punta Arenas to Cape Horn. The idea was for him to shoot a lot of action footage to make the documentary more exciting, and to cover angles and situations that were impossible for Margaret and me to film.

We put on additional stores in Punta Arenas and met Admiral Eduardo Allen who was the head of the navy in the south. On April 17 we welcomed the photographer and his wife, who we will call Adam and Eve. We set off at once and retraced our route south along the Strait of Magellan,

One day we had a visit from Admiral Eduardo Allen who was the commander of the Chilean naval forces in the south.

and then sailed south and west along Magdalena and Cockburn Channels to the western end of Tierra del Fuego.

Again we were surrounded by high mountains, but now at 55° S the low trees—what there were—leaned severely to the east, wedge-shaped as if trimmed by giant shears. The rock was grayer and more fractured and rounder than further north, evidence of increased glaciation. Most of the place names had been given by Fitz Roy and the crew of the *Beagle*. We passed Islas Stewart, Londonderry, Hamond, and Whittlebury, for instance.

A few days later we sailed into the northwest arm of Beagle Channel where, in a distance of twelve miles, five large glaciers descended from the north side of the mile-wide channel directly into the water at sea level. It was a fine experience to glide slowly along in front of glacial snouts of fissured blue ice that extended upward for hundreds of feet. I say "hundreds" but the ice seemed miles high. Streams of icy water ran down the fronts and there were eerie grumbling and grinding noises as the ice inched forward. We fished out fragments of ice floating in the channel and had great sport fixing cool drinks. It was all so beautiful that we spent two days taking photographs and walking on shore.

Now we were within striking distance of Cape Horn and I was determined to make a fast run for our goal. We were technically bound from Punta Arenas to the Chilean naval base at Puerto Williams. Permission for Cape Horn had been on a "yes you can," "no you can't" basis, and I was worried that we might be denied permission at the last minute on some technicality or other. We had learned that South America was full of technicalities.

On April 28 the four of us aboard *Whisper* pushed hard and made it to the north end of Canal Murray, only seventy miles from Isla Hornos. It was now the end of April and the hours of daylight were short because we were well into the southern autumn. The next morning I got everyone up in the dark and we were underway by 0815. We hurried south-

(Overleaf) The western end of Isla Tierra del Fuego seemed a world of gray stone and primordial beginnings. Whisper's sails made a dot of white on a landscape so vast you could scarcely fathom the immensity of this wilderness world.

ward through Canal Murray, dipped our flag to the Chilean lookouts, and sailed southeast.

The day was gray and overcast and the clouds to windward looked ragged and full of squalls so at 0910 Margaret and I tied a reef in the mainsail and put up a smaller headsail. Meanwhile Eve steered and Adam took photographs. At 1025 we were running well before a freshening northerly wind as we sailed away from the snowy mountains of Isla Navarino and out into the open waters of Bahía Nassau. Ahead, rising from the horizon, we saw the dark forms of Islas Wollaston and Hermite, an archipelago with eight good-sized islands, on the southernmost of which was Cabo de Hornos. I could hardly believe the sight. Was this Cape Horn at the foot of the American continent? The fabled and awesome sailing hurdle of centuries? The air was clear, and on Isla Hermite, twenty-five miles away, I could plainly see the tops of a row of bare mountains which stuck up like the teeth on a saw blade.

Margaret wanted to go to the Hardy Peninsula and anchor in Bahía Orange, which was closer and supposedly a good anchorage. I overruled her, however, and chose to head for the Wollaston Islands, a little further to the southeast, and only twenty-four miles north-northeast of Isla Hornos. The *Pilot* books suggested three places in the northern part of the Wollaston Islands: the first was Surgidero Otter, an anchorage for large vessels in ninety-two feet but open to the north. The second was Surgidero Romanche in fifty-three to one hundred five feet, fairly well sheltered, but not recommended because of violent squalls from the mountains on Isla Bayly during westerly gales. The third was Surgidero Seagull, described as being well sheltered and suitable for small vessels of reduced draft. Since the soundings were moderate—which promised less work recovering the ground tackle—and the anchorage was surrounded by islands, I selected Surgidero Seagull. From this anchorage we would be in an excellent position to sail around Isla Hornos during good weather. In addition the approach to Cabo de Hornos from the east would mean that we would be sailing in sheltered waters and should have an easier trip. Also there were more protected harbors on the east sides of the islands.

Our progress was good, but I was concerned about the barometer which had dropped from 997 millibars at breakfast time to 984 by mid-afternoon. We were now sailing fast under the running rig before northerly winds of twenty to twenty-five knots. During a routine gybe while running, I winched in the sheet of the headsail whose clew was held outboard with a spinnaker pole (as I had done a thousand times before). Suddenly the pole collapsed where it pressed against a forward lower shroud. We quickly replaced the broken pole with a spare and resolved to treat aluminum poles more gently in the future. Certainly the thin metal poles should not be subjected to bending strains.

By 1500 we had logged forty miles and were rapidly approaching the Wollaston Islands which consisted of four irregular islands, mostly volcanic, that measured about twenty-five miles from northwest to southeast. From a distance the islands looked brown and bare. Mount Hyde, the highest point, rose to 2,211 feet.

At 1700, Eve reported that the barometer had plunged to 979 millibars, an ominous nine o'clock position, and I knew we were in for a blast from the west. Adam and I dragged a second anchor to the foredeck.

The approach to Seagull anchorage was from the south. I was surprised when we entered because instead of a snug cove we had come to a low basin a mile and a half in diameter. Above us to the west rose the smooth slopes of Isla Bayly. It was obvious that winds would roar down from the island and race out across the anchorage. Even worse was a mass of kelp in the mostly twenty-six-foot depths of the bay. The kelp was as thick as water lilies in a pond.

We had worked out anchor bearings from the chart and *Pilot* so we hurried to the recommended place and dropped the anchor. We began to drag in the twenty-knot northerly wind so I winched up the anchor and found some gray mud on it, along with a ball of matted kelp which I cut away. I let go the anchor a second time. Again it dragged. This time it came up with no mud at all—only a huge sphere of kelp. I hacked away the weed and dropped the anchor a third time. Then a fourth. The autumnal night was descending rapidly.

In lowering clouds and darkness, Margaret took bearings of two mountains. We seemed to be holding, but I had misgivings about what might happen with the low barometer so I let out all the chain on the first anchor and put out a second anchor on a long nylon line.

The north wind began to veer toward the west. I could hear the williwaws begin to race down the mountain on Isla Bayly. A few minutes later we were enveloped in seventy-knot winds. Initially the sound was like screaming sirens. But as the wind increased and gradually swung to the southwest, the roar changed to the low-pitched whine of giant turbine wheels. The noise was a bus engine running at full throttle inside my head.

I peered out of the hatch. Sheets of spray slammed into my face. All landmarks had disappeared. The only thing I could see was the white tracery of excited water flying over the yacht. I thought of moving to a deeper anchorage. I thought of another anchor. I thought I'd never heard such wind . . .

Suddenly we felt *Whisper's* keel grate on the bottom. The yacht fell hard on her starboard side and crunched into rocks. Water came in at once.

We were shipwrecked on uninhabited islands only a few miles from Cape Horn.

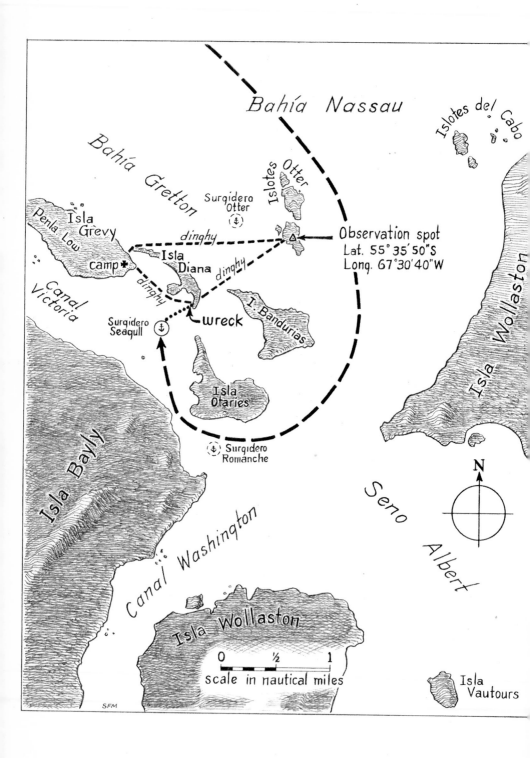

Bahía Nassau

Islotes del Cabo

Bahía Gretton

Islotes Otter

Surgidero
Otter

Observation spot
Lat. 55°35'50"S
Long. 67°30'40"W

Isla
Grevy

Penla Low

dinghy

camp

Isla
Diana

dinghy

dinghy

Canal
Victoria

Surgidero
Seagull

wreck

I. Bandurias

Isla Wollaston

Isla
Otaries

Surgidero
Romanche

Seno
Albert

N

Isla Bayly

Canal Washington

Isla Wollaston

0   ½   1

scale in nautical miles

Isla
Vautours

SFM

NINE

Shipwreck

THE FIRST feeling the shipwreck gave me was one of incredulity. "It can't happen to me," I muttered as I bit my lip. "Wrecks only happen to other people, because *my* preparations and *my* seamanship are too perfect." Yet poor *Whisper* lay wounded on a rocky beach on an uninhabited islet twenty-four miles north-northwest of Cape Horn. At high tide the yacht was one-third full of water, and the pounding of the hull against the cannonball-sized rocks was no myth.

Each incoming wave picked up the vessel a little and dropped her as the water receded, slamming the yacht down on the beach. The hull creaked and groaned and shivered. It was awful. I thought of all the places Margaret and I and *Whisper* had been together—French Polynesia, Rarotonga, Samoa, Kusaie, Japan, the Aleutian Islands, Alaska, the Queen Charlotte Islands, the Galápagos, Peru. . . . We had had a few dangerous moments but *Whisper* had always come through. But now, stupid fool, I had let her down. The mighty captain had allowed his vessel to drag ashore in a heavy westerly gale. The whole thing was monstrous and inconceivable.

(Overleaf) Shipwrecked in the Wollaston Islands near Cape Horn.

Shipwrecked! Obviously the anchors had gotten fouled and were useless. Could I lay out another anchor on a long warp? I looked out into the inky night. Bursts of frigid spray slapped me in the face like shotgun pellets as the waves broke on the stony beach where *Whisper* lay thumping. At that moment another barrage of williwaws exploded down the mountains of Isla Bayly. The moan of the wind quickly increased to a baritone wail. There was no possibility of launching a dinghy and putting out an anchor until the wind eased.

According to the angle-of-heel indicator we lay at fifty degrees to starboard. The visibility was terrible but by waving a flashlight around I could dimly see that we were on the edge of an islet with smooth water only a few yards to leeward. Maybe we would blow or bump our way across. But as soon as I thought of this I knew we would never move to the quiet water beyond the islet because the yacht was so firmly aground. Indeed, the starboard deck almost touched the beach which was composed of smooth, roundish stones eight inches or so in diameter. There were hundreds, no thousands of these stones that clattered together when a wave rolled in, and again a moment later when the water ran out. It was hard to look around because of the flying water and the steep angle of heel of the yacht. It took a good deal of hanging on to keep from falling over the side.

If only I could row an anchor out to windward while the tide was still flooding. . . . I wondered how many shipwrecked mariners had muttered those words?

To keep from getting increasingly soaked with cold water as the waves broke over the yacht I went back inside and slammed shut the hatch. Below, I found water rising inside the hull. We had no doubt been holed or stove in on the starboard side where the yacht was pounding. The date was April 29; the time was 1930. We still had two and a half hours to high water. I made a quick calculation with the tidal tables and worked out that the water would rise less than two feet, not enough to swamp or submerge the vessel.

It was impossible to walk around inside *Whisper* because of the angle of heel. We climbed from handhold to handhold. All the loose gear tended to fall toward the low side which was soon a couple of feet deep in the water. I thought of the women chatting quietly about dinner half an hour earlier. Now we had to shout to talk above the noise of the wind, the waves, and the pounding of the hull. Everything had happened so quickly that I was only vaguely aware that a new chapter in my life had begun. I knew that hard times lay ahead.

There were four of us on board. My wife Margaret, dear Margaret, was as steady as a pillar of stone and completely dependable when the going was hard. Eve—the photographer's wife—had sailed with us for a few days in California at an earlier time. She seemed sensible, calm and thoughtful, full of ideas, and she was always willing to pitch in and help. I had no idea how she would react in a crisis.

I knew less about Adam, her husband. He was a big, well-built man with a huge beard and a deep bass voice. A talented film maker, he was smart, his mind was logical, and he spoke well. In the last few days I had learned that he knew little about sailing and was hesitant about helping with the yacht and various chores unless I directed him step by step. Although he wanted to learn about long distance sailing he considered any sort of detail work—making eye splices and whipping the ends of a halyard, for instance— as "women's work" and "boring" and simply refused to do it which I thought odd. How Adam would act when the going got tough was anybody's guess. I hoped for the best.

We were in a nasty situation. Yet it was far from hopeless. Fortunately the yacht was being battered by relatively small waves because the opposite shore of Seagull anchorage was only a mile and a half away. With limited fetch the waves had little time to build up. The accident had occurred about three and a half hours after low water and what waves there were had shoved us well up on the beach. This meant that we would be high and dry at low water. It would be easier to work on the yacht but harder to get the vessel down to the water to refloat her. Patching the hull and hauling the yacht into the water were not my concerns just then because the refloating would need calmer conditions.

Our biggest problem was exposure and cold. The diesel stove was submerged in salt water; the cabin was soon to be one-third full of 39°F water. All of us, however, were warmly dressed in woolens, oilskins, boots, hats, and gloves. Most of the bedding was dry. The yacht was cold but she gave us protection from the wind.

"We'll stay here until morning," I announced. "Let's turn in and get some rest."

Adam and Eve crowded into the quarter berth which was on the high side of the yacht. Margaret and I managed to nap on the port saloon berth which had a large canvas lee cloth. I fired up the one-burner Taylor kerosene cabin heater which happened to be on the port side. I climbed into the angled saloon berth, intermeshed my oilskinned limbs with Margaret's, and managed to doze a little. The heating stove flue didn't work too well because of the high wind. I wondered whether I should get up and shut off the stove. "Is it better to die of asphyxiation and be warm, or to be cold and alive?" The stove hissed away and I fell asleep pondering the question.

I awoke from time to time because my position was so cramped. In the night the tide fell and the water drained from inside the vessel. The pounding of the hull on the beach stopped. The silence was wonderful. I climbed outside. Though the wind was still strong, the spray was gone. I took a flashlight and dropped to the beach. I wanted to see where we were and I was curious about the land, but the low clouds made the night very dark and my seaboots slipped on the mossy rocks. The walking was treacherous. I went back to the yacht to wait for daylight. The others were still asleep.

At first light I dropped to the beach again and walked around the yacht. Except for a chunk torn from the bottom of her rudder, *Whisper* seemed in good condition. The entire port side was perfect and looked as if the vessel had just come from a shipyard. The damage, however, was underneath the starboard side on which she lay. I was amazed to discover that the second anchor we had dropped the night before was up on the beach higher than *Whisper*. In fact the anchor had been blown or carried by the water across the end of the islet to the extremity of the nylon cable which was stretched tightly downwind. Think of the power of a storm to do that!

We were on Isla Diana, a scimitar-shaped islet about one mile long and a quarter of a mile wide on the west side of Seagull anchorage. The islet was only about ten or twelve feet above the sea. There were no trees, only large clumps of tall, coarse-leaved tussock grass. Across from us to the west and south rose the brown and withered mountains and hills of the main Wollaston Islands. Patchy snow lay near the heights.

It was impossible to prepare anything to eat on board so we took a Primus stove and some food to the lee side of the islet. The wind kept blowing out the Primus so we got the yacht's dinghy and dragged it around the islet for a windbreak. Margaret cooked hot cereal and made coffee. I took a couple of pictures of *Whisper*.

After eating, Adam and I walked along the slippery beach stones to the opposite end of the islet to have a look at our general situation. While we were picking our way across the rocks, Adam suddenly stopped and turned toward me.

"What are our chances, Hal?" he blurted out. "I mean, do you think we'll ever get out of this?"

I had been so busy thinking about the wreck that I hadn't paid much attention to Adam. Now, when I looked closely at him, my heart sank. He was shaking in his boots. His eyes had become slits and he was almost crying. Instead of looking at me when he spoke, Adam looked at the ground. During World War II and the Korean War, I had seen what fear could do to a man. The stranding of the vessel was bad enough. To be obliged to deal with a terrified photographer who had an acute case of the browns was trouble indeed.

"The yacht is finished," he said. "We don't even have a radio. How much food is there? I want an inventory of the food right away. We must count the cans."

"Relax," I said. "Margaret and I have done a lot of mountaineering. We know how to live out in the wilds. The yacht is extremely well provisioned and we have enough food for at least two months. If necessary we can supplement the food with shellfish. We may have to find some fresh water."

"Water?" said Adam nervously. "How much is there? How many days will it last? How much can we have each day? Let's sound the tanks right away."

I tried to reassure him. "I think we can get the yacht off," I said. "At least we're going to try hard. When the wind drops we're going to run out a couple of anchors, move a lot of stones, and see if we can turn the bow toward the water. At high tide we may be able to slip a couple of drift-wood timbers under the starboard side. Then at the next low tide when the hull is empty of water we'll try to bolt a plywood patch on the hull. We may have to work in the water a little. I have a thick rubber wet suit . . ."

"Work in the water?"

I saw that Adam was horrified. It was clear that he wanted nothing more to do with the yacht. His idea of heaven just then would have been for the clouds to open and a helicopter to land and whisk him to the Cabo de Hornos Hotel in Punta Arenas, 188 miles to the northwest.

Back on the yacht Eve and Margaret had taken more food ashore and we all had a hot lunch on the beach. Then, while I worked inside to expose the hull damage, I asked Adam to take the dinghy and row out an anchor. The wind had dropped and the job was easy. I told him exactly what I wanted, but when I looked out later I saw that he had put the anchor out to the south, not the west. A fifteen-minute job had taken two hours and instead of securing the anchor warp to the port bow cleat to help pull the yacht toward deep water, Adam had put the warp on the starboard stern cleat which meant that he was tying the yacht to the land. Maybe on purpose. Poor Adam was wandering about in a daze.

We had thousands of feet of new 16-mm film and two cameras on board. "How about taking some footage of the wreck and what we're doing?" said Margaret to Adam during the afternoon. "After all, a photographer doesn't have this opportunity every day."

"You're entirely right," said Adam in his deep bass voice. "We must start on a systematic shooting schedule and chronicle every aspect of this experience. We need a lot of good sequences."

Adam talked eloquently but he took no photographs— then or in the days to follow. Later he climbed into the yacht where I was working. He was looking for something and began to pick up things from the high dry side and let them fall into the water on the low side of the saloon or the galley. He took a large plastic jar with all my taps and dies and drills from a tool drawer that I had open. His eyes were searching for something else so he simply dropped these irreplaceable tools into the salt water. I gasped. I could hardly believe what I had seen. At first I was angry, but as I moved closer to shout at him I saw that Adam's eyes were glazed and that he was breathing heavily. He was sick with fear and not in control of himself. Instead of anger I began to feel sorry for him.

I took Margaret aside and spoke to her privately. "Adam is pretty upset," I said. "He's in a bad way. We're going to have to set up a camp on shore and forget about *Whisper*."

Margaret had been watching Adam on her own and she agreed with me.

I gathered everyone together and spoke in strong terms for Adam's benefit. "Tomorrow morning, if the wind is down, Margaret and I will take the fiberglass dinghy and row across the hundred yards or so to Isla Grevy, the next island, to see about setting up a camp in the grove of trees that Adam and I spotted this morning on our walk. I know from reading that Indians and seal hunters have lived in the Wollastons, and I believe we'll find water and shelter. We can make a tent with the sails from *Whisper*. Tonight we'll stay on the yacht, but by moving a few things we can be more comfortable. It's possible that we may see a patrol vessel or a fishing boat. In addition, I think there's another Chilean navy lookout station south of us. I don't know whether it's on Isla Hermite, Herschel, or Deceit, but we may find something. So everybody cheer up. Let's all have a whisky and then some dinner."

The next morning Margaret and I rowed across to Peninsula Low on Isla Grevy. We found a good-sized rivulet of fresh water, and in walking through the trees we discovered the remains of an old campsite. A conical tent of some kind had once been arranged over a framework of poles. The tent was long gone but the framework was good enough for us to throw a sail over for shelter. The camp was about thirty or forty feet above the water; a walk of one hundred fifty feet to the north took us to the eastern edge of the peninsula where we had an excellent view north and northeast into Bahía Nassau and of Isla Navarino in the distance beyond. Lots of wild celery grew near the camp. Margaret saw mussels that uncovered at low tide.

During the next few days we rowed several dozen loads of sails, bedding, bunk cushions, tools, line, water jugs, dishes, and pots and pans to the camp, which gradually became quite deluxe. We lashed three sails around the existing tent framework to make a serviceable tepee which we floored with sail bags and the sun awning. Then came cushions and mattresses followed by blankets and sleeping bags. We had two kerosene stoves and a pressure kerosene lantern. There were several hundred cans of food plus larger containers of flour, rice, sugar, noodles, and spaghetti. We dug a shallow ditch around the tent to drain off water and gradually improved the tent with props and lines until it was quite weatherproof. I am sure the sailmaker would have been amazed to have seen what we had done with his handiwork.

Eve worked especially hard collecting mussels which she steamed, fried, curried, or made into delicious soup. She hauled water from the rivulet and gathered wild celery. At first her husband wanted a big nightly campfire until we convinced him that wet wood would make a smoky fire besides being a lot of trouble to get going and keep up. Adam liked the camp but he still acted nervously. He slept at least ten hours a night and spent hours writing furiously in a notebook. We repeatedly asked him to use the movie cameras, but nothing happened.

It is not my purpose to mock Adam and to make sarcastic

Our good-rowing Davidson dinghy was invaluable in exploration and for moving supplies and food.

comments on his behavior, but simply to observe that when fear grips a man it changes him and he becomes wretched and useless. Adam was the biggest person in the party and he should have been the strongest. Fear bled his strength away and he became the weakest.

We tried to assign Adam little jobs. Not much seemed to interest him, however, until Margaret got the idea of giving him the rifle and making him the camp hunter. Adam was a good shot and disappeared for hours on hunting expeditions. He brought back big kelp geese which Eve cooked in the pressure cooker. The meat was dark brown, something like turkey, and it tasted delicious. The trouble was that the thirty-thirty rifle was much too powerful for birds. The big slugs tended to destroy the creatures instead of merely killing them as a shotgun would have. Nevertheless, we were glad for the additional food, even if it was in small pieces.

Working to set up the camp and running it was a full-time job and a half. Collecting naturally occurring food may sound romantic but it takes an unbelievable amount of time and patient effort unless you are a local native and have learned to do it from childhood on. We saw lots of clam shells along certain beaches but we had no rake, which I thought of making from a deck brush and a row of copper nails.

The weather was surprisingly mild. A few days were stormy, but in general the wind and cold were minimal. Maybe we were getting used to Cape Horn living. Of course once on land we tended to ignore sea conditions.

We spent many hours rowing back and forth to the wreck and carrying things across the slippery rocks. The round trip was about two miles or so, but part of the way was through kelp whose long, heavy stalks and leaves would get wrapped around the oars. The person rowing would have to stop, unship the fouled oar, slide it out of the kelp

Unloading supplies on Isla Grevy with the Wollaston mountains in the distance. The moss-covered rocks along the shore made the walking treacherous.

(or cut the leaves away), and then re-ship the oar and begin again. It was always easier to go around kelp patches even if it meant a long detour.

One morning when Margaret and I started out for the wreck I got the idea of rowing along the outside—the northwest side—of Isla Diana to avoid the heavy kelp. The wind was calm and I thought we might see something new along the beach. We started out well but the kelp was thicker

The emergency camp on Isla Grevy was based on this tent made from sails wrapped around poles set up tepee fashion. We were reasonably protected from strong winds in this grove of small trees. We found fresh water, wild celery, and mussels nearby.

than I had foreseen and the rowing quickly became impossible. Every two or three strokes I had to unship the oars to clear them. All of a sudden, gusts of wind from the southwest began to blow at us and to push the dinghy away from shore. I re-doubled my rowing efforts but I only got the oars fouled twice as fast. At first our position was merely annoying, but it quickly grew alarming. Here we were in a tiny dinghy only eight feet long getting blown away from land! I threw out an anchor at once, but it didn't hold in the slippery kelp. I had read somewhere about Indian women mooring canoes by tying to bunches of kelp, so I knelt in the bow of the dinghy, grabbed three or four thick kelp branches, and passed a line around them. The line slipped from the slimy stalks. I tried a second time. The line slipped again.

All this while the wind was increasing—say, to thirty knots. Not a great deal, but in a small dinghy even a little is a lot. We were gradually losing ground and getting blown to sea. I looked shoreward to see if there was any chance of help. Adam and Eve stood watching us, not knowing what to do. I tried to wave to them to send us a float or the inflatable dinghy on a long line, but the notion didn't occur to them in spite of my earnest gestures. I remember so well thinking of two expert sailing friends in San Francisco and wishing that one of them had been on the beach to help us.

Margaret and I were rapidly getting blown away from shore. What to do? I glanced behind us. Fortunately there was another islet about a mile to leeward. Whether we would be able to make our way there, however, and to land in one piece were questions that I couldn't answer or even think about. Already we were skimming along downwind in swells higher than the dinghy's freeboard. I found that by keeping the stern exactly parallel to the swells, we went along in fairly good fashion. I steered by using the oars as drags, digging one in a little to turn the vessel slightly. It was a delicate business and my heart was in my mouth because if we had gotten broadside to the waves we would have capsized at once, and certainly would have perished in the frigid water. Margaret sat perfectly still in the sternsheets and gave me directions as we steered across the swells toward the islet.

The sea got lumpier and we raced downwind. I was afraid that we would be swamped any second. Finally, as we got near the islet, and close to the rocks and small breaking waves on the lee shore, Margaret spied a little sheltered place past a tiny bit of land. We avoided several rocks, managed to steer past a stone ledge, touched bottom, jumped out, and quickly ran the dinghy high up on the shore. I almost wilted from nervous excitement. If there hadn't been an islet to leeward we would have been blown out to sea east of Cape Horn.

During my life I have been lucky to sidestep death many times, but this was the most providential. As I guided the dinghy by selectively dragging the oars, I remember thinking of a book by John Muir in which he described the first ascent of Mount Ritter in California's Sierra Nevada in 1871. Muir had been climbing for hours and he finally got into a situation in which he could neither go up nor come down. He clung high on the side of the mountain with his arms outstretched while noisy ravens chattered nearby. "Not yet, not yet," he cried. "I'm not carrion yet."

"Not yet, not yet," I mumbled to myself. "We're still alive, even though we passed through the shadow . . ."

Margaret and I walked around and around the little islet—its name was Islote Otter, we later found out—for the next eight hours to keep warm. We ate some mussels from tidal pools and collected tiny red berries from bushes. At dusk the wind dropped and we were able to launch the dinghy and row back to the grounded yacht for a load of gear. We then returned to the camp on Peninsula Low and stumbled into the tent in the dark. Adam and Eve had put out the camp light and had gone to bed. Eve got up to fix us something to eat.

"We thought you had bedded down for the night," she said.

"Bedded down?" said Margaret. "Bedded down in what?

If we had bedded down on the islet we'd have died of exposure."

Seagull anchorage was discovered in April 1839 by the 110-ton New York pilot schooner *Seagull* which was part of the U.S. Navy exploring expedition led by Charles Wilkes. Unfortunately, a few days later the *Seagull* left Bahía Orange on a routine voyage and got into a furious gale. The *Seagull* (two officers and fifteen men) was never seen again. In November 1855, W. Parker Snow, the energetic captain of the eighty-eight-ton missionary schooner *Allen Gardiner*, anchored in Bahía Gretton and took a ship's boat into Seagull anchorage. Snow noticed a deserted wigwam and he walked ashore at the precise site of *Whisper*'s emergency camp on Peninsula Low. During the same week, Snow and the *Allen Gardiner* went through a five-day hurricane plus squalls that almost tore his schooner apart. He lay with two big anchors out, one on 540 feet of chain.

During the night of the third day of its prevalence, I was on deck when a furious squall of hail and wind, similar to a tornado, burst upon us with a force like the blow of an enormous sledge hammer. The little ship trembled again; you could hear every part of her move under that tremendous blast, and I might easily fancy her a living thing shuddering with the apprehension of the wrath and power of those terrible elements she was calmly striving to resist. On that wild coast, near that dark and frowning land, during that inky night relieved occasionally by fitful gleams of a strange and peculiar light, with the large hail pelting upon one like showers of bullets, I could not but feel deeply anxious.[27]

Louis-Ferdinand Martial, in charge of the 1882–83 French scientific mission, visited Seagull anchorage to chart the region and discovered that Victoria channel ran between Isla Bayly and land to the north. Martial named the separate land Isla Grevy, "in honor of the first magistrate of the Republic." In 1923 the artist-adventurer Rockwell Kent sailed to the area in a small chartered boat from Ushuaia.[28]

All four of these visitors—Wilkes, Snow, Martial, and Kent—found Indians living and working on the islands. A little seal hunting, fishing, and shellfish and crab gathering supported the people in subsistence fashion. The account by Rockwell Kent is charming. Kent even contrived to baptize the half-breed offspring of an Argentine ex-prison inspector and a Yaghan woman.

We in the *Whisper* party thought it a pity that the lives of the Indians had been so tampered with by the missionaries and white settlers. The Indians were all dead—gone forever. We would have liked to have seen them and to have learned from them how to live off the land.

Adam and Eve and Margaret and I began to make reconnaissance hikes to the west and north of the island. Two of us went out on each clear day to see if we could find any people or structures or shipwrecks or a campsite closer to Peninsula Hardy or Isla Navarino.

The land was severe, but it had redeeming qualities. Isla Grevy was mostly open and rocky, with handsome light-brown coloring. Parts of the island were boggy and you had to watch your footing to keep from stepping into little pockets of sphagnum moss. Our routes climbed through flats of matted brush and dwarf wind-blasted trees. In protected canyons and draws along the shores we walked through luxurient thickets of evergreen beeches twenty-five to forty feet high. These small forested areas always had water, tall grasses, wild celery, and thick topsoil. In every one we visited we saw traces of Indian campsites.

We found no animals. The only land birds were a brown mockingbird type about ten inches long with white horizontal lines above and below the eyes. Along the shores we scared up lots of steamer ducks which would rush off, madly flapping away, and leave wakes of foam behind. I was never sure who was startled more—the steamer ducks or I. We saw many kelp geese about the size of small turkeys. The females were a hard-to-see mottled brown. The males stood out in white dress with specks of black. If you saw a male you could be sure that a female was nearby, but it took hard looking to spot her. We noticed a few brown ducks, some seagulls, and black cormorants with white breasts.

Along much of the shoreline of Grevy were large rounded boulders covered with slippery moss. Half in and out of the water, the big rocks guarded the shore like tank traps and made walking extremely hazardous. The combination of the boulders and masses of nearby offshore kelp made any small-boat work unthinkable.

From heights on the island we looked out across at Peninsula Hardy, eight miles to the west. With a sky of blue, the water was blue too, and the sunny Pacific seemed lovely. Below us, at our feet, lay Bahía Beaufort which was wide open to the southwest swell; even from a distance the water had a feeling of power and purpose. From the north end of Grevy we could see across the thirteen miles of Bahía Nassau toward the snowy slopes of Isla Navarino which shimmered in the blue haze of distance.

By now a week had passed. I removed a heavy twelve-volt storage battery from the wreck and took my English Aldis signaling lamp to the lookout point past the camp. The powerful light was visible for fifteen miles—perhaps more—so we signaled from time to time toward Isla Navarino which we knew had some ranches on it. Eve got the idea of spreading a sail on nearby dark trees in case a plane flew over. I began to work on a sailing rig for the dinghy.

On the ninth morning Margaret and I started rowing to the yacht when we saw Adam and Eve run through camp. Adam had my Olin flare gun and began to shoot red and white flares, all of which fizzled out after rising only a foot or two. We hurried to the lookout point and saw a Chilean torpedo vessel about three miles to the northeast.

I grabbed the Aldis lamp and called up the Chilean vessel. She stopped at once and I signaled our identity and condition. Margaret had the binoculars and reported that a rubber boat was being launched. Adam was whooping with joy.

"I'm glad to see the Chileans too," said Eve, "but I'm a

little sad that our camping experience is over. I would have liked to have explored a little more."

Twenty minutes later an officer and three Chilean sailors waded ashore. I ran up to the man in charge and apologized

Another view of the emergency camp looking southwest across Seagull anchorage to Isla Bayly. The growth of shrubs and grasses is surprisingly lush in the southern autumn. We see jugs of water, the U.S. flag, and a few camp chores in progress. We found many signs of earlier camping, presumably by Indians.

, for his wet legs and feet.

"Oh it's nothing," he said, his face all aglow. "These patrols are a bore. Rescuing someone is the most exciting thing that's happened to us in years."

TEN

Salvage

THE 118-FOOT Chilean navy torpedo boat *Quidora* picked up the four of us from the emergency camp in the Wollaston Islands and whisked us around the east end of Navarino Island to the Chilean naval base at Puerto Williams. As Captain Raul Ganga completed the sixty-mile trip and eased his vessel into the dock that fronted on Beagle Canal, it seemed that half the people on the base had come down to see us. Everyone treated us with great courtesy, almost as if the shipwrecked mariners had been snatched from the jaws of death. The most disappointed man was a medical aide from the hospital who had expected us to be suffering from hunger, malnutrition, and grave injuries. We thanked him for his concern but assured him that we were all in good condition and well fed. "Plenty of good Chilean shellfish down there," said Margaret.

The commander at Puerto Williams, Fernando Camus, was a tall, handsome man with fair coloring who looked more like a Dutch naval officer than the head of a military base near Cape Horn. Camus spoke flawless English, and—

Seagull anchorage and Isla Diana in the Wollaston group twenty-four miles north-northwest of Cape Horn. A chalupa with fifteen men is being rowed from the Castor *to the wrecked yacht on shore.*

like the captain of the torpedo boat—was full of charm and confidence. We met briefly with newspaper reporters and television cameramen and then were taken to a small guest house. This was all very nice, but I was terrified at what might be happening to poor *Whisper* languishing on the beach of Isla Diana. News of the rescue was out on the radio and I feared that every fisherman and freebooter within a hundred miles would be converging on the wreck to strip her.

"The yacht represents all my assets," I said to Commander Camus. "I'm worried sick."

"You forget," he replied, lifting an authoritative right forefinger. "You forget that the navy exercises absolute control of this area. No one is going to bother the yacht. If the weather cooperates we're going to help you."

An hour later I was introduced to Lieutenant Horacio Balmelli who was the captain of the *Castor*, an eighty-two-foot workboat that was used for various supply and general utility jobs. Messages had been going back and forth to Admiral Allen in Punta Arenas and a plan developed to send the *Castor* to refloat *Whisper*, or at least to salvage her gear. Everyone was taking a personal interest in the refloating. It was a good sign and immensely reassuring.

Balmelli and I spent several hours discussing refloating schemes and salvage materials. He wanted to take along scuba divers, but I told him our need was for timbers, plywood, wedges, picks, shovels, sledgehammers, a few fifty-five-gallon oil drums, a pump, and a lot of bolts. "The yacht is high and dry on the beach at low water," I said. "If we can expose the damaged side we may be able to bolt or screw a patch over the damage."

Balmelli shook his head. "Machine screws and sheets of plywood are very difficult to get in this remote place. You might as well ask for gold bars or watermelons. Let me think about it, however, and I'll look around the warehouses."

On May 9, two days later, we were back at Seagull anchorage. The *Castor* had been joined by the *Fuentealba*, a slightly larger workboat. We had a great pile of salvage materials plus the twenty-five men of the two crews.

By now I had gotten to know Horacio Balmelli—the commander of our little two-ship expedition—a bit better. A graduate of the naval academy in Valparaiso, he was a quiet Chilean who had been stationed at Puerto Williams for four years. He and his family loved the peacefulness of the south and the opportunity to take long walks together in the absolute wilderness. Sometimes when he was fishing along a stream he would look up and see half a dozen fleet-footed guanacos watching him. Although Balmelli was a professional mariner, his mind had the steplike logic of an engineer, and he seemed happiest making plans for some project or other, complete with major objectives, alternatives, and contingencies. His ambition was to start a U.S.-type coast guard in Chile, and he was keen to study search and rescue techniques in America. Balmelli joked with me about the story of the last two men on earth. One was Argentine; the other was Chilean. Their food was gone and they had only a few hours left.

"What were they talking about?" went the line. "Girls? Money? Sports cars?"

"Heavens no," said Horacio. "They were arguing about the border between Chile and Argentina."

Balmelli was sympathetic to my plight with *Whisper* and he was optimistic from the beginning. "We're going to get her off," he kept repeating. "We're going to get her off." It almost became a litany and soon was taken up by everyone on the *Castor*. "We have another secret weapon," said Balmelli. "My bosun, Oluf Torres, is a Chilote and a clever fellow if there ever was one."

The two workboats anchored about a third of a mile from the wreck. Each vessel carried a six-meter tender called a *chalupa* that was rowed back and forth to Isla Diana with men and supplies.

My idea to recover the yacht was to dig under the starboard side, to slip timbers under the hull, and to through-

205

bolt or screw plywood patches on the inside and outside to make a firm sandwich repair. Then, after some pick and shovel work to smooth the beach, I hoped to turn the bow toward the water by laying out two anchors and taking a strain on the warps at high water. At this time I could check the hull for watertight integrity. Finally, after more beach smoothing at low water, I would skid the vessel in at high tide.

Balmelli's scheme was to erect a steel A-frame (borrowed from the navy base) over the yacht and to lift her slightly with a set of compound tackles in order to expose the damaged side enough to patch it. He then planned to lay the yacht on a special cradle for small vessels (also borrowed from the base) and then to drag *Whisper* into the water.

While Balmelli and I discussed the merits and disadvantages of our plans, Torres slipped ashore with a few men and took charge. Starting at the stern he put a small hydraulic jack under a strong point on the hull and lifted it two inches or so. He then tapped in a timber and a wedge to hold what he had gained with the jack. Torres then moved a few feet forward and lifted the hull again and inserted another small timber and a wedge. He worked little by little and gradually the hull began to straighten up. Initially the yacht lay at fifty degrees, then forty, and then thirty, and finally at eighteen degrees, securely held by timbers and wedges and several empty fifty-five-gallon oil drums. The work of Torres and his men was impressive. Balmelli and I abandoned our plans and bowed to a superior performance.

I got inside the hull and cleared out several dozen large stones, a couple of hundred pounds of gravel, and a mass of slippery kelp. I took a wrecking bar and a light sledgehammer and ripped out the entire galley, the dinette, the starboard seats, stowage lockers, and shelves. By the time I got down to the hull itself the area had been raised above the beach and enough light came through the rupture so that I could see the extent of the damage. The fiberglass hull had

Torres in charge. Note the small hydraulic jack near the transom of the yacht. The beach is composed of fine and coarse stones up to about eight inches in diameter. The Castor *and* Fuentealba *are anchored in the distance.*

an evil-looking U-shaped tear that measured forty-seven-inches long in a horizontal direction. At the forward end the tear turned vertically upward for eight inches. At the after end the tear rose twenty-six inches. In general the hull was a hell of a mess. Nevertheless we saw that if the rupture could be bridged by structural material and padded to make it watertight the vessel would be seaworthy.

In viewing the damage objectively, it was remarkable that the wreckage wasn't worse. The hull had pounded on rocks at each high tide for eleven days. A wooden hull would have been kindling. A steel or aluminum hull might only have been dented.

The weather turned nasty. A cold wind blew from the west. The men wore heavy clothing; some had on woolen face masks. One of the *chalupas* had gotten broadside to the surf while landing and had turned over. Several of the men had gotten soaked. But everyone's morale remained high. As is the custom in these regions a bottle of *aguardiente* was passed around. We all took a gulp of the fiery brandy which was good for a little instant heat and perhaps a momentary mental lift because the work on the beach was truly a grubby job. At high water the sea lapped around the keel and it was impossible to work in the frigid, swirling water. With the hull raised, however, the interior was safe from flooding.

I realized that my behavior was paramount to the success of the mission. I made it my business to be on top of all the action. I got acquainted with the men and learned some of their names. I pulled on the leading oar of *Castor's chalupa*. I jumped ashore in the surf before the others. I passed out tools. I discussed problems with the officer in charge of the *Fuentealba*. I worked inside the hull. I carried hot food ashore. I spoke with Torres. I schemed with Balmelli. I pitched in entirely, not only to work but to lead the work. Again and again I asked: "What can I do to help?" I don't quite know where I found the energy for all this but it came from some hidden resource. I realized that this opportunity was my only chance to get the yacht off the beach and I wanted to spread my enthusiasm to everyone. Also I had no idea how long the navy would support the salvage operation. It could be stopped at any moment. We had to work quickly!

The only sour note in our efforts was Adam, the photographer. Margaret and Eve had had to stay behind at Puerto Williams because there was no place on the workboats for women. Adam asked to be taken along. "I'll photograph everything and I want to break down the camp and help bring our things to Puerto Williams," he said. In a moment of weakness I agreed. But as I feared, Adam did neither

Timbers and wedges were used to hold the yacht as she was lifted by the five-ton hydraulic jack. (Below) I soon learned to appreciate the usefulness of scrap timbers, wedges, and old oil drums. Whisper's hull at 40°.

of his announced jobs. Instead he stood around looking nervous or was asleep ten or eleven hours out of twenty-four. Unlike everyone else, he did no work of any kind and conveniently missed taking down the camp (which I and four Chilean sailors did). The Chileans recognized that Adam was disturbed and acting oddly. "Why doesn't he do something?" I was asked again and again. "The mental stress has been too much," I replied weakly.

Lieutenant Balmelli had managed to bring along a large sheet of half-inch plywood from a packing box. The plywood was soggy and not the best quality, but it was strong and could be bent slightly in two directions—just what we needed. I passed a hand saw to Torres who cut an L-shaped patch that overlapped the hull damage by two inches or so. Meanwhile I ripped out some insulating carpet from the interior. The idea was to pad the plywood with carpet to help smooth the rough places and to serve as a kind of packing. At first I had planned to bolt the patch in place with half-inch or five-eighths diameter machine screws, but these were not available. After thinking about the problem I realized that quarter-inch stainless-steel machine screws were adequately strong and that I could increase the bearing area on each side of the patch with large washers. A sailing friend in California, Lou Goaziou, had given me a good supply of such fastenings and I blessed his generosity.

A sharp quarter-inch drill bit in an eggbeater hand drill easily cut through a piece of half-inch backup plywood, the hull, the carpet, and the plywood patch itself. Torres pushed in a bolt from the outside, and eager fingers put a washer and a nut on the inside. Then a second hole and a second bolt. We faced the complication of bending the patch slightly in two directions—over the vertical curvature of the hull and around the fore and aft curvature as well. This required some levering with timbers. The patch, pulled down bolt by bolt, slowly closed over the hull wound. A dozen hours and two tides later the patch was securely held by an encircling ring of forty-eight bolts. Someone then

Torres marks the damaged area and decides on the size of the
plywood patch. (Below) The patch partially bolted in place. Note
the padding of carpet between the hull and the plywood.

caulked the edges of the patch with cotton. Torres smeared thick plastic paint over the entire repair. The color even matched the hull.

In Chile and Argentina, vessels under fifty feet are often taken from the water on an *anguilera* or cradle. This is made in two parts, a port half and a starboard half, each contoured to fit the bottom of the hull. While the vessel is in the water, the halves are floated into position on each side and securely chained together. A cable from a powerful windlass is led to one end of the cradle and the whole works is dragged longways up a shipyard ramp. The cradles are generally made in twenty-five-, thirty-five-, and forty-five-foot lengths. The curve of the cradles need not fit a hull exactly because the contours can be padded with sacks of

The patch has been completed and has been caulked and painted. Torres is checking the tightness of the forty-eight bolts that hold the patch to the hull.

straw or bundles of rags.

We had brought along the starboard half of a thirty-five-foot cradle and now dragged it in place alongside the patched hull. Torres did a little work with his hydraulic jack and drove in a few wedges and timbers and soon the yacht rested on the cradle ready for the water. We spent a few hours moving stones and smoothing the path to the sea while four men in a *chalupa* brought a hawser in from *Castor*'s windlass. At high water, Balmelli signaled *Castor*. The engineer turned on the windlass. The cable tightened but the yacht didn't move an inch. Again Balmelli waved his signal flags. The windlass strained and strained but nothing happened. Everyone was glum. I felt like death.

Suddenly we saw some movement on *Fuentealba* which was lashed alongside *Castor*. The lieutenant in charge had the hawser belayed on *Castor*. He then fired up the main engines on both work vessels and put them in forward—full speed ahead! *Whisper* lurched, skidded sideways a few feet, and then plunged smoothly into the water. She was afloat!

During the salvage we had used most of the Dacron and nylon lines that had been on board *Whisper*. After the yacht was in the water we gathered all the tools and timbers and line on the beach and rowed them back to *Castor*. Unfortunately a large box with most of the lines and warps was dropped overboard. The coils of irreplaceable line sank into the depths, a bitter loss that was to trouble us for months.

Eighteen hours later the yacht was in Puerto Williams after a fast tow by *Castor*. Margaret and Eve met us on the dock. *Whisper*'s interior was a sopping shambles of broken wood, soaked clothing, wet charts, squishy sails, ruined books, and rusting tools. Yet everything was aboard and we were thankfully afloat.

Some unseen keel damage caused the yacht to leak badly. I had to pump three hundred strokes an hour. And—as many mariners have learned to their sorrow—leaks don't stop at sunset. The next day Margaret and I and Torres used *Castor*'s cargo boom to unstep *Whisper*'s mast. We said good-

Whisper *rests on a cradle or* anguilera *as a hawser is led from the* Castor *to the wooden framework. (Below) The yacht slides into the water as the two lashed-together workboats gun their engines and pull ahead to assist* Castor's *deck winch.*

bye to Adam and Eve who climbed into a DC-3 and flew homeward. Two days later the Chilean naval vessel *Águila* docked to unload supplies for Puerto Williams. On her return trip north she was to take the yacht to the shipyard in Punta Arenas. There was no shipping cradle for *Whisper* and no materials to make one, so a masterful Chilean bosun simply picked up the vessel in a cargo net and deposited the yacht gently on her side on a bed of old tires laid on deck. An impossible operation you say? I agree completely, but it was done—at night and in a swirling blizzard.

I was near collapse from the mental strain and all the pumping. A steward led me to a cabin as the *Águila*'s deck lines were cast off. "We get the funniest cargo sometimes," he said. "A *yacht* is on board. Now what would a little sailboat be doing down here?"

Arrival at Puerto Williams on Isla Navarino after a tow from the Wollastons by Castor.

ELEVEN

A Giant Repair

OUR RESCUE from an uninhabited island near Cape Horn returned us to civilization, but we faced a monstrous problem. Quite simply, it was to repair a gaping big hole in *Whisper*'s hull, to fix the keel, and to renew the rudder in a city that was eight thousand miles away from the boatyard where the yacht was built. In addition, every bit of gear on board was soaked with sea water, much was streaked with mud and rust, and some was missing altogether.

The yacht was unloaded from the navy ship and taken out of the water at the Asmar shipyard in Punta Arenas on the Strait of Magellan. Several hundred men worked at the shipyard, which was a military–civil service operation that dealt chiefly with Chilean naval vessels, a few local fishing boats, and did some commercial work. While we were there, the *Monsunen*, for example, a steel coasting vessel from the Falkland Islands, came in for repairs and painting.

The men in the yard were cordial and certainly curious about *Whisper*, but in truth they were terrified of her—perhaps as heavy truck mechanics might be nervous about working on a Ferrari or Porshe sports car. Fortunately I knew the

Whisper goes into the water after her ride from Puerto Williams to Punta Arenas aboard the Águila.

yacht inside and out and was well acquainted with fiberglass repairs. I planned to be on hand every minute and to supervise all the work.

Our first project was to take the bedding, books, bosun supplies, charts, clothes, cooking stoves, cushions, dishes, foodstuffs, hardware, lines, medical supplies, navigational equipment, papers, pots and pans, the rifle and revolver, sails, spare parts, toilet articles, tools, my ukelele, and a hundred other bits of gear to a small apartment the navy had loaned us. Everything needed to be washed and cleaned and dried out. To move all these wet belongings required three trips of a fair-sized truck and emphasized once again the quantity of living and sailing equipment necessary for distant voyages. For shipyard stowage we got two enormous wooden boxes into which we put the anchors and warps, bilge pumps, chain, compasses, the depth sounder, engine parts, fire extinguishers, and so on. In addition, we loaded the boxes with all the broken galley and saloon woodwork that I had ripped out in the Wollaston Islands and had piled in the forepeak. It seemed incredible how much stuff we took from the yacht. We needed three days to get the inside cleared out.

The cabin sole and starboard side were still deep in mud. I borrowed a hose and pump from the fire department, put on my boots and oilskins, and signaled a man to turn on the water. I had to laugh at myself. When we had set out for Cape Horn I had never thought that I would ever be standing inside the cabin with a fire hose washing out mud, gravel, and kelp. I have learned, however, that surprise is the nature of world voyaging. Every day is different. You never know what is coming.

Half an hour later I had all the mud and pebbles washed to a central spot. We reversed the pump, sucked out the water, and suddenly the interior of the ship was clean. *Whisper* seemed naked and exposed, but at least we had begun.

The Asmar shipyard was the only repair facility in the south. The Chilean navy ran the yard and had generously

offered to repair the yacht free of charge. "We have a tradition of helping people down here," said our friend Admiral
Eduardo Allen who was in charge of the navy in southern
Chile. "Within the limits of the yard capabilities we want
to put your *Whisper* back into seagoing condition."

The shipyard men had taken the yacht from the water
on May 20. So far one week had passed. I had been given
three weeks to get the entire job done and the vessel back in
the water. Already the newspaper reporters were demanding
a launching date. The difficult hull repair, unfortunately,
hadn't even been started. Re-equipping the yacht seemed a

The hull damage to Whisper's *starboard side was suddenly
exposed after the patch put on in the Wollaston Islands was
removed. The damage was serious, but after pounding at each
high tide for eleven days it was surprising that the problems
weren't worse. The resiliency and strength of the fiberglass hull
were remarkable.*

distant nightmare. No one at the yard seemed to be in the slightest hurry.

Winter was a month away. The days were getting short. The weather at 53° 10′ south latitude was cold. In order to repair the fiberglass hull we would either have to erect a heated tent around the hull or put the yacht inside a heated building because at freezing temperatures the polyester resin would never harden.

Due to the language problem and my unfamiliarity with the shipyard, a man named Juan Espinosa was appointed to "coordinate all efforts." Espinosa was a pleasant, middle-echelon civil service worker—always courteous and nicely dressed—who spoke some English. I used to think that he looked old until one day I found out that he was exactly my age, which was a real shocker. Espinosa was sincere, dedicated, and well acquainted with the various department heads, but even he sometimes shook his head when confronted by the quagmire of civil service politics. "We all have to be patient," he said to me one morning when I was upset that something hadn't been done as promised. "Don't worry," he said. "We are all working for you."

I discussed the concept of time with Espinosa. If an American or Englishman or German said 0900 he meant 0900. But to a Chilean or Peruvian 0900 meant 0930, 0945, maybe 1000, or, God forbid! even 1100.

"Suppose a navy ship was attacking the enemy," I said. "I suppose the torpedoes wouldn't be ready until tomorrow."

Espinosa smiled and laughed: "Oh that's quite different. It is just the normal custom to be a little relaxed about close timing."

With winter approaching, the best plan was to move the yacht inside the torpedo building, a large, heated, all-weather structure. "It is very secret," said Espinosa in a whisper. "The building is full of classified war materials. No one is allowed inside. You can see the sign and the guard yourself."

"What sort of torpedoes are inside?" I asked. "American?

French? English? German?"

"English torpedoes," said Espinosa. "But don't say I said so."

"English? Well then pass the word," I told him. "Margaret was a petty officer in the British Royal Navy during World War II. Certainly if . . ."

"I will tell them," said Espinosa, hurrying off.

Whether Margaret's background had any effect I don't know, but that afternoon the yacht and her cradle were dragged along a trail of greased timbers into the torpedo building. Whisper's mast, boom, spinnaker poles, two dinghies, and the two large wooden storage boxes followed, all piled up against some decrepit English torpedoes that were covered with thick grease. At last we could start to work.

I knew that it is difficult to make major fiberglass hull repairs because it is hard to duplicate the original curves. Strands of fiberglass saturated with wet polyester resin have about the same rigidity as wet noodles. A form or mold is necessary—either on the inside or outside—to hold the wet fiberglass until the resin sets up and the material begins to display its amazing strength and form-holding ability.

Whisper's starboard side midships was a mess. Her port side, however, was in perfect condition. But a mold taken from the good side would have been a mirror image of what we needed. I had two willing carpenters, Luis Ocampo and Hector Chavez, who cut nine vertical hardwood frames spaced ten and a half inches apart on the port side exactly opposite the damaged starboard side. We then reversed each frame by turning it 180 degrees about its vertical axis. We tacked each frame in place on the starboard side by using spacers between the frames and several long battens to hold the whole assembly together. Now we had a pattern for the starboard side. Ocampo and Chavez then took down the form and tacked sheets of thin pressed board on the inside. This was covered with wax so the new fiberglass wouldn't stick to the mold.

The next step was to cut away the hull damage, a large

The first step was to cut nine vertical frames to match the hull contours on the undamaged port side. Each frame was then revolved 180 degrees on its vertical axis and put on the starboard side where it was held in place by spacers and battens as we see here.

The framed structure was then taken down and its inside contours were covered with thin pressed board to make a mold. Notice the torpedoes in the background.

section of smashed fiberglass about seventy inches long and thirty-five inches high. The edges of the opening were carefully ground so that a long taper was left to ensure adequate area for a good bond between the existing hull and the new material. We then fastened the mold to the hull with a few bolts and were ready to put on the fiberglass.

While Ocampo and Chavez were working on the mold, I had removed the structural bulkhead between the saloon and the galley on the starboard side. This bulkhead was in the way of the repair and needed some fixing of its own.

All the work at the shipyard was on metal or wooden

The damaged hull section was cut away and the edges of the opening were carefully tapered to ensure ample area for a good bond. The saloon-galley starboard bulkhead has been removed. (Below) Layers of mat and roving were laid up from the inside with ample overlaps over the existing part of the hull.

hulls. No fiberglass vessel had ever been at Asmar before. It was fortunate that Ocampo and Chavez occasionally repaired fiberglass life raft containers and their mounts, and understood how to work with resin and glass. I had some fiberglass mat and roving material and a few gallons of resin on board. We managed to get more. Ocampo dragged in several cylinders of bottled gas and fired up a big blowtorch-type heater underneath the hull to raise the temperature. One morning we had a mad fiberglassing scene as layers of mat and roving were alternately laid in place and saturated with polyester resin. To strengthen the patch we glassed in three longitudinal stringers which overlapped both the old and new work. A few days later we installed the repaired starboard bulkhead and glassed it in place.

While all this was going on we had streams of visitors even though the torpedo building was supposedly secret and restricted. Every day most of the shipyard workers managed to detour past the yacht to see what we were doing. We got to know the secretaries from the shipyard office. We saw tourists, visiting brass, merchant seamen, fishing boat crews, and of course the officers from the navy headquarters in town. The newspapers wrote frequent progress reports. The television cameramen were forever shooting film. Some of the visitors thought that the patch would fall off; many were in agreement that the yacht would never leave the torpedo building. A few thought the yacht might float. But no one dared to think of going around Cabo de Hornos *in that!*

While the hull, keel, and rudder repairs were underway, Margaret worked hard taking loads of clothes and bedding to the laundry. She had hundreds of books and papers spread around the apartment drying; clotheslines were strung everywhere for special projects. She cleaned every piece of galley gear and removed thick rust from most of my tools and many of the spare parts. There were no replacements to be bought, so, like the Chileans who saved everything, we learned to make do with what we had. Margaret spent hours cleaning rust from engine oil filters, for example,

After the resin had set up we removed the mold. Here with a powerful light inside the hull you can see the outline of the longitudinal stringers (overlapping the old and new work) that we added for strength. The general appearance is a mess, but the hull is as strong or stronger than when the yacht was built originally. Only grinding and filling and cosmetic painting remain to be done. When completed there was no trace of the patch and it was impossible to tell where the yacht had been damaged. Later on, for fun, we told people that it had been the other side of the hull— the port side—that had been damaged, at which point one of our visitors generally said "I can see it," which was baloney because the port side had never been damaged at all. The object at the lower left in the photograph is not a machine gun but a space heater fueled by bottled gas.

and wire-brushing corroded Primus burners for the kerosene stoves. She dunked rusty cans of food in fresh water, dried them, and then wiped each can with oil.

We desperately needed line to replace the lost halyards and sheets, and we wanted new injectors for the diesel engine. These things were not easily available so we sent off to the U.S. and Sweden. Regrettably, the parcels never arrived.

When we left Punta Arenas we had to be self-sufficient for three months. This required a considerable stockpiling of food which was costly in inflation-ridden Chile. Margaret went from store to store with her lists and shopping baskets. To buy flashlight batteries and woolen gloves required visits to a dozen shops. The stores had an astonishing amount of German goods. It seemed that a couple of German super-salesmen must have passed through Punta Arenas. We saw German bread-slicing machines, tools, towels, barometers, packages of dried soup, sleeping bags, detergent, radios, bedsheets, even cuckoo clocks—dozens of things and all from Germany.

Our Punta Arenas sojourn wasn't all drudgery. Sometimes new acquaintances invited us to their homes for meals. We got wonderful letters of encouragement from friends in the U.S. and Canada. Margaret managed to fit in a few lessons of Spanish, which she enjoyed immensely. Often at noon we walked to a small shop in the center of town where we bought freshly-made *empanadas*, a delicious Chilean speciality of spicy beef or chicken, olives, raisins, onions, and a slice of hard-boiled egg, all baked together in a crispy pastry envelope.

Every morning I got up in the dark and stumbled through the sleeping city at 0630 on my way to the shipyard. Fortunately I had my hiking boots on board so I had good footwear to walk along the dirt roads and across the frozen puddles. Sunrise in June wasn't until 0915; sunset came about 1645, so I got used to walking home in the dark.

As soon as the hull was closed up I began to assemble the galley and saloon. There was no new wood available so I used the wreckage I had torn out earlier. It is amazing how you can glue smashed wood back together. Epoxy glue, splints, and a couple of screws can do wonders. I had no time or materials for a fancy job. I needed to get *Whisper* operational quickly.

Even so, it was impossible to have the yacht ready by the yard deadline. On June 13 Espinosa told me that *Whisper* was to go into the water on the following Wednesday. "Impossible," I said. "She is in no way ready for sea. It will take several days just to step the mast and rig her. The interior is still a shambles." The next morning I asked the navy for two more weeks which was granted. I was requested to leave the torpedo building, however, so over the weekend Margaret and I did some fast cosmetic work on the patch and hull and quickly slapped on topside and bottom paint. On June 18 the yard men moved the ship from the torpedo building and took her to the launching ramp. Heavy snow was falling so we hurried to install the diesel stove and to fire it up for warmth.

I put the repaired alternator, starter-generator, and injectors on the diesel engine. Margaret glued insulating carpet on the inside of the hull repair. I collected the two storage batteries, put them on board, and began to hook up the new wiring on the starboard side. Espinosa and I made a trip to the machine shop to collect the welded spinnaker pole and the straightened lifeline stanchions. Two bronze stanchion bases had been crushed almost flat, but a clever welder had managed to reconstruct them.

One day at noon Margaret appeared with all the upholstered cushions, which had been specially cleaned and dried by the Modelo Laundry. We got the saloon table mounted. A repairman delivered my two typewriters in good working order even though they had been submerged in salt water for two weeks—a real miracle. One afternoon I mounted the galley sink, hooked up its drain pump, and installed the fresh and salt water taps. We borrowed a truck to move all the dried and cleaned gear from the apartment.

Although the exchange rate was 720–780 escudos to the dollar, we spent money at an alarming rate. Starter-generator bearings cost 8,500 escudos; injectors were 26,000 each; one set of foul-weather gear was 35,000. The laundry bills totaled 66,000. Three new Chilean *Pilot* volumes were 26,400 escudos. The charges for a 250-foot nylon warp totaled 40,000. Every time we went to the food shops for stores we spent half a dozen crisp green 5,000-escudo notes. The inflation rate was 1 percent a day and in a store it was a race to buy goods with marked prices before the clerks could change the figures.

When we stepped the mast the usual yard gang of twenty men showed up. Three or four would have been ample but the Asmar shipyard worked by the platoon system and there was no changing it. I bolted on the boom gallows, hooked the main boom to the mast, and hoisted a Chilean courtesy flag that had been presented to us by Rafael Gonzales, the captain of the *Orompello*, in a particularly pleasant little ceremony. *Whisper* was beginning to look seaworthy.

Our sails were still covered with thick mud from the camp in the Wollaston Islands. For a month we had tried to find a large, clean, paved area with running water so we could scrub the sails and inspect the stitching. Finally our friend Peter Samsing introduced us to a colonel in charge of a nearby army barracks who offered us the use of a big shower room. Unfortunately, on the day we arrived with the sails the officer was away and had forgotten to tell his sergeant about us.

Can you imagine two foreigners speaking pidgin Spanish arriving at a heavily guarded armory in a snowstorm and trying to get over that they wanted to wash sails? The confusion was total. But we kept at our story. Finally a corporal recognized us from the newspaper stories. Suddenly there were torrents of laughter and smiles all around on the former stern and worried faces.

Whisper's launching was simple because we were already on a cradle. We slipped into the water and chugged out to an enormous mooring buoy and tied to it with three lines. Right away I knew I was going to miss the bleating of all the transistor radios. The frustrations during the seven weeks in the shipyard had sometimes seemed more than a human could bear. Like civil service operations in the U.S. and England, Asmar appeared to be ready to capsize from the weight of its top-heavy brass, its paperwork, and endless talk. Yet I don't want to complain because I was an invited guest. I will always be grateful for everything that was done for Margaret and me. If there be any complaint maybe it is that Americans are too hard driving, too impatient, and too demanding of deadlines and promises. Maybe we should be more relaxed and loose and try to emulate the charm of the Chileans. But then how can a launching dead-line—or any other—be met?

I felt so alone at times. No one had any idea of the enormousness of the job we had done on our tiny yacht. We had crammed three months' work into seven weeks. The results weren't perfect and lots of work still remained, but by God we were afloat and operational. We had managed to sidestep shortages, to outmaneuver red tape, and somehow to keep pressing on. Margaret had been wonderful—always optimistic, encouraging, and full of resolve. Of course the whole repair job was my fault in the first place because I had let the ship drag ashore in a storm. . . . How tired and weary I was. I felt like a knife blade that had been ground down to the handle on an abrasive wheel.

Suddenly I heard an engine roaring alongside. I looked out to see a large steel launch bearing down on *Whisper*. Espinosa and the Asmar chiefs plus reporters and photographers and their various women friends were coming to see us. Crash! We frantically put out fenders and tried to push the bow of the launch sideways to get the invasion force alongside and stopped, but the driver gunned his engine in reverse, backed off smoothly, and prepared to attack again. Crash! The inexpert helmsman smashed his battering ram into our bow. Crash! Now our stern. Crash! And crash again! Couldn't one of the officers aboard the launch tell the driver to come alongside parallel and at slow speed?

I tried to wave off the launch. Everybody smiled and waved back. The television cameramen were shooting film. I feared that our fragile eggshell would be sunk on the spot if the launch persisted in striking us. We were helpless. The steel projectile circled for a try from a new direction, came alongside, and we threw them bow and stern lines. Everybody scrambled on *Whisper* for a thorough look. The women clucked at the galley and the reporters asked the usual questions. Espinosa proudly lectured the Asmar chiefs about what had been done. We were filmed from all directions. We shook hands with everyone, received their blessings, and finally the launch was gone.

"I think it's time to get the clearance and to head south," I said to Margaret. "One more onslaught like that and we'll have to swim ashore. Certainly Cape Horn will be easier."

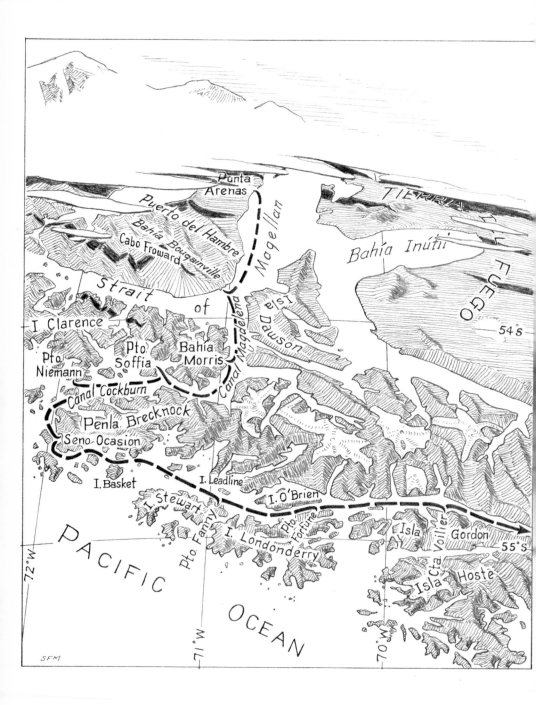

Punta
Arenas

TIERRA

Puerto del Hambre

Bahía Bougainville

Cabo Froward

Strait

of

Magellan

I.Dawson

Bahía Inútil

DE

FUEGO

54°s

I.Clarence

Pto.
Niemann

Pto.
Soffia

Bahía
Morris

Canal Magdalena

Canal Cockburn

Penla. Brecknock

Seno Ocasion

I.Basket

I.Leadline

I.O'Brien

Pto.
Fortune

I.Stewart

Pto. Fanny

I.Londonderry

Isla

Isla Cta. Voilier

Gordon

55°s

72°w

71°w

70°w

PACIFIC

OCEAN

Isla

Hoste

SFM

TWELVE

South Again

*W*HEN WE SAILED from Punta Arenas on July 14 for the second attempt at Cape Horn the yacht was barely seaworthy. Margaret and I were exhausted from the seven-week ordeal in the shipyard. We needed a quiet place to rest for a few days and time to complete dozens of small jobs on *Whisper*. We had anchored in Bahía Bougainville twice before, so we immediately sailed forty-three miles south along the Strait of Magellan to the west side of the strait near Cabo Froward. As before, we found the little bay quiet and isolated and pretty with its dense thicket of surrounding beech trees that climbed steeply upward from the rocky shores.

Captain Louis de Bougainville discovered the tiny bay that carries his name in 1765 when he was collecting wood for the Falkland Islands (which were then controlled by the French and called the Malouines). He returned two years later with the frigate *la Boudeuse* and the store ship *l'Étoile* on his way to Tahiti. Bougainville had learned to moor his ships if possible, and he ordered each of his vessels to drop two anchors and to run hawsers ashore to the trees.[29]

Since we had already been blown out of the bay three and a half months earlier and had later suffered our terrible accident, we dropped two stern anchors as soon as we arrived. Then we rowed ashore two strong bow lines which we tied to stout beech trees. During the next two nights the west wind blew hard. When I looked out at the windy black void into which I couldn't see as far as my fingertips, I felt a bit apprehensive. How good it was to have lines ashore to windward in those southern anchorages!

While waiting for an improvement in weather before sailing south along the Strait of Magellan we tied up to this old four-masted iron-hulled barque in Punta Arenas. The dim outline of Tierra del Fuego is across the water to the left.

I mentioned earlier that the yacht was barely seaworthy. Her hull, ground tackle, engine, sails, and interior were all right. The problem was the rig and the crew. We had stepped the mast but the yacht had been launched before I got the rigging adjusted and the turnbuckles secured. I wanted time to rig the spinnaker poles, to install a repaired staysail halyard block, to fix the spreader lights, and to complete many small jobs. The yacht desperately needed to be scrubbed and cleaned. Margaret and I hoped to have a couple of days of rest.

During the salvage at Seagull anchorage we had lost a large box of lines and now were very short of halyards, sheets, and warps. I had tried to have 600-foot spools of half-inch Dacron and five-eighths-inch nylon sent from the U.S., but the shipment never arrived. The only line available locally was three-quarter-inch yellow polypropylene (which was too large for *Whisper's* blocks), and some rather inferior quarter-inch manila (which was much too small and weak). After wondering what to do I got the idea of cutting our few remaining Dacron sheets and halyards in two and lengthening each half by splicing on a long tail of quarter-inch manila to make up for the missing Dacron. We then did the initial hauling on the quarter-inch manila to take up the slack of a sheet or the easy part of hoisting a sail. By the time we got to a heavy strain on the line we were past the manila and the splice and down to the strong half-inch Dacron.

While we were in Punta Arenas I had asked the captain of a cargo ship for a nylon anchor warp. The captain had no nylon but he generously gave me 325 feet of inch and five-eighths diameter manila line. It was heavy and intractable stuff but it served us well. At first the manila was stiff and covered with grease and dirt. After a month of use in clean salt water, however, the line became supple and bleached and reminded me of the braided hair of a Swedish girl.

We sailed south into Canal Magdalena and west along Canal Cockburn. It was now midwinter and there had been

(Overleaf) Monte Sarmiento from Canal Beagle. This prominent peak, named after the early Spanish explorer, is seldom visible because the prevailing westerly winds tend to build up dense clouds around the mountain. Only in easterly weather—not too common—does the double summit appear and then only briefly, giving rise to picnic weather and sunny skies.

a dramatic increase in snow since our first trip. It was easy to tell the times of high and low water because of the snow line at the water's edge. Though the weather was cold, the sailing was magical and we traveled in a fairy world. The mountains of Tierra del Fuego to the south rose up white and gigantic above the dark water. Sometimes the wind blew streamers of snow from the high ridges and peaks. These snow banners blew to leeward for hundreds of feet and made incredible ribbons of white that waved like giant hoists of celestial flags. The winter sun shone low from the northern sky and pinned its reddish rays on snow scenes that flickered before my eyes like the unreal images of a dream.

Margaret and I wore layers of woolens for warmth, and waterproof oilskins for protection from the wind and spray. We kept our heads and ears warm with woolen caps. I put on two pairs of thick hand-knitted woolen stockings inside my seaboots and wore woolen gloves inside large rubber gloves. We alternated short watches of an hour or two.

Each night we moored carefully. Sometimes we stayed over for a day, and gradually got both rested and well into the list of jobs on the yacht. We installed the stanchions and lifelines, repaired the broken cockpit spray dodger, and made new flapper valves for a bilge pump from scraps of a rubber inner tube. The carburetor for the diesel stove never functioned properly after its dunking in salt water, so I finally scrapped the valve and fitted a simple drip feed device, which fortunately worked well. I finished making a spare tiller because the emergency tiller had gotten broken in the accident. The galley sink drain needed a gasket. I braced a weak settee front with two battens and a dozen screws. We spent one day scrubbing the decks and cockpit floor trying to remove an accumulation of mud, soot, grease, rust, resin, and paint from the shipyard.

Near the western end of Canal Cockburn we sailed into Puerto Niemann, an extremely remote and seldom-visited anchorage at the southern end of Isla Clarence. The land was low and partially bare with windswept trees that leaned to the east. As we approached the area I took bearings of various points but none of the land forms shown on Admiralty chart 554 made any sense. I scratched my head and looked again. Margaret, who is good at coastal pilotage, came on deck and was puzzled too. I soon realized that the chart reflected utter fantasy and showed "Duntze islands and channel" where in fact none existed at all. The Admiralty *Pilot* was vague and unspecific. We immediately got out Chilean chart 1201 which was quite accurate and reassuring. Margaret read aloud from the Chilean *Pilot* V which had proper descriptions.

As we jibed and sailed into Puerto Niemann—who was Niemann?—I had the distinct feeling that no one had ever been in the anchorage before. There was no sign of man and I had the eerie premonition that if we had a mishap ashore our anchored vessel might not be discovered for a dozen years. I half expected to see pirates or pixies, Spanish galleons, or green men from Mars. For the real loner this was the ultimate place. Never had I sensed such isolation and remoteness.

The anchorage was well sheltered with good holding ground, but we got into a mess. I elected to anchor near the western shore because of the usual westerly winds. We dropped a stern anchor and headed toward land until the line was taut. I then took the dinghy and started to row a bow line ashore. While rowing the line to the beach, however, a squall funneled down from the land and began to blow me, my warp, and the yacht away from the shore. I rowed harder, furiously, and was only a few feet from shore, but it was no use. Normally this would have made little difference because I would merely have been blown back to the yacht which was anchored. At Niemann, however, the holding ground for the anchor was steeply shelving and in a minute or two the dinghy and I, the warp, the yacht, and her stern anchor —now hanging straight down in deep water—were all blowing merrily downwind.

I shouted at Margaret to give a little forward boost with

During the eight months of our stay in the Chilean channels we filled our water tanks again and again by pouring water into jugs and then ferrying them to the yacht via the dinghy.

the engine, but *Whisper* was drifting astern faster than Margaret realized and the slack from the stern anchor line got into the propeller.

Pandemonium! We had no engine. It was getting dark, and strong squalls of sleet hurled down from the western shore. I rowed back to the yacht in record time and pulled up the stern anchor. We then made sail and beat back very close to the western shore where we anchored. I got two lines ashore and carried out a second anchor. Safe at last!

The lesson I learned was always to carry a line ashore to a windward shore *before* dropping an anchor on a steeply

shelving bottom.

The next morning we tried various schemes to free the line from the propeller. Nothing worked. I put on my wet suit very reluctantly, a bit afraid of the cold water because we had seen chunks of ice in Canal Cockburn. Once in the water, however, I unwound the warp from the propeller in a minute or two and scrambled back on board. The fear of the icy water was far worse than the water itself. I was ashamed of myself for being so slow to go in. Actually I felt wonderful afterward.

To the north-northwest of us at the southern end of Isla

Santa Inés was Seno Dresden, a long, skinny, west-facing fjord that had been a hiding place of the German light cruiser *Dresden*, a survivor of the 1914 naval battles of Coronel and the Falkland Islands. When World War I began, the German China squadron under Admiral Maximilian Graf von Spee steamed eastward to South America. Initially, von Spee had two powerful heavy cruisers which were later joined by three light cruisers.

To oppose this German thrust into the southeastern Pacific, England lined up an armed cruiser, two light cruisers, an auxiliary cruiser, and a decrepit old battleship, the *Canopus*, which could only steam at twelve knots, half the speed of the other vessels.

The Battle of Coronel took place off the central Chilean coast on November 1, 1914, with both fleets steaming southward into a heavy sea and a strong southerly wind. The Germans outmaneuvered and outgunned the British and sank both the flagship *Good Hope* (with Rear Admiral Sir Christopher Cradock) and the *Monmouth*. On December 9, five weeks later, von Spee attacked the Falkland Islands, which he planned to seize and turn into a German base. But the British had reinforced Port Stanley with two large battle cruisers which had been sent at full speed from England and which had arrived only twenty-one hours before von Spee appeared. With Admiral Sir Frederick Sturdee in command, the two big British ships (with twelve-inch guns) plus four light cruisers came out fighting and after a spirited battle sank four of the German men-of-war. Those killed included Admiral von Spee and his two sons. The only ship to escape was the *Dresden*, which fled to the southern Chilean channels where she played a cat-and-mouse game with British cruisers. In March 1915 the *Dresden* steamed to Isla Juan Fernandez where she was sunk by the British cruiser *Kent*.

Reading about these naval actions more than sixty years later, it is hard to realize the problems of fuel and communications. Few ships had wireless sets in 1914, radio direction finding was unknown, there was no aerial reconnaissance, and the big naval vessels used dozens of tons of coal each day and had to be met by fleets of colliers that had been arranged for ahead of time. But the men were tough. Their patriotism was strong and direct even if the motives of the war were clouded. The worst part of the two battles was that some two thousand sailors in the flower of their manhood were killed to little purpose except for the vanity of two countries.[30]

We sailed around the western end of Tierra del Fuego where the gray land met the Pacific. We looked at a brittle world of half-drowned mountain summits, a battleground where the restless water collided with the tops of the Andes which here were near the sea. Most of the land was bare and climbed from the water in massive curves and billows of glaciated stone not long removed from an ice age that had ground the sharp summits into soft surves. A few scrawny trees clung together in heroic clumps whose tops were shorn by the westerly gales. The great swell of the Southern Ocean crashed on a miscellany of rocks and ledges and islets with stunning force, flinging the shattered water high into the air. Captain Robert Fitz Roy, the first man to chart this area, named the region the Milky Way because of its resemblance to the night sky. "The chart of it, with all its stars to mark the rocks, looks like a map of the heavens rather than part of the earth," he wrote aboard HMS *Beagle* on January 27, 1830.[31]

It was wildly exciting to sail in such a place. But the needle of our barometer was skipping downward in large nervous jumps. We hurried into well-sheltered Seno Ocasión on Peninsula Brecknock as the wind began to rise.

While stormbound I wrote in my journal:

July 20th The view outside is a study of grays and dark greens; of giant granite domes fringed at the bottom with small trees; of noisy waterfalls and cascades trumbling from high overhead; of mist and blowing rain and then periods

of quiet; of curious small birds that dart on deck and peer in at the portlights and companionway; of perfectly smooth water that is clear and dark and cold; of black and white cormorants nesting above us who glide and swoop and flutter when returning home and then sit like waxen sentinels for hours, scarcely moving. The air is crisp and hard and almost tingles with purity. Ashore not a sign of man. No footprint or rubbish heap. No hut or tottering fence or rotting boat. I finger a bush with berries; a vine with small red flowers; a dwarf tree as high as my hand. I take a squishy step across a tiny meadow of sphagnum moss. From the top of a rise we look at a series of small lakes, each dropping into a lower until the last topples into the sea and is gone. Overhead the clouds run swiftly eastward, pushed by the vigorous wind from the west.

Captain Fitz Roy gave names to locations as they were mapped. Places were named after men on the expedition, for famous people, because the place suggested a name, or due to some incident during the survey. As we sailed eastward in *Whisper,* now south of Tierra del Fuego, we passed Seno Courtenay, Paso Adventure, Cabo Fletcher, and Islas Catherine, O'Brien, and Gilbert, all good British names.

The patience and tenacity of Fitz Roy and his men during the tedious survey work in the square-rigged *Beagle* and in open whaleboats was astounding, and the accurate charts are remarkable monuments to the skill and determination of these English sailors. Poor Fitz Roy had one problem after another. One hundred and fifty years ago the Cape Horn region had a population of perhaps five thousand highly independent and clever Indians. While anchored at Isla London, for example, Fitz Roy sent a whaleboat and seven men to an island fifteen miles away. During a stormy night Indians stole the whaleboat. The men from the *Beagle* managed to contrive a sort of basket boat by weaving small branches together and covering the basket with canvas and mud. Three men somehow rowed the basket boat back to the *Beagle* and gave the alarm.

Fitz Roy immediately set out with another whaleboat to recover the stolen boat. At a nearby Fuegian camp the men from the *Beagle* discovered the missing whaleboat's mast. Encouraged, the party pressed on and two days later found the whaleboat's leadline in a camp some twenty miles to the east. A friendly Indian took the party to a nearby cove where the men of the *Beagle* recovered more boat gear. Fitz Roy was convinced that the cove was the home of the thieves. The Indians led the Englishmen on a long and frustrating wild goose chase for nineteen days. Fitz Roy retaliated by taking Indian hostages and their children, but the crafty Indians slipped away and left Fitz Roy to look after the children. In the end, the *Beagle's* carpenter had to build a new whaleboat.

Now in *Whisper* we sailed along Whaleboat Sound (Canal Ballenero) and passed Isla Basket (named for the basket boat), Isla Leadline, Cabo Longchase, Isla Hide, Thieves Sound (Seno Ladrones), Bahía Escape, and Thieves Cove (Caleta Ladrones). We almost felt the presence of Fitz Roy and his trusty crew. Where was that damned whaleboat anyway?

FOURTEEN

Final Triumph

*A*LTHOUGH the westerly gales sometimes blew fiendishly hard near Cape Horn there were plenty of sailing days when the wind eased to ten or fifteen knots. The light winds generally came with a morning cloud level of three hundred to five hundred feet that cleared as the day progressed. *Whisper* was south of the big island of Tierra del Fuego and we headed eastward and made good time in pleasant conditions, often under full sail. As we glided along in smooth water in the lee of small islands, the world around us seemed still and quiet. Our existence was a mote of nautical dust amidst a galaxy of snowfields and mountains and waterways.

The date was July 22, the middle of winter. It seemed a bad time to be heading for Cape Horn. True, the hours of daylight were short, but it was well documented that the winter weather was better. The most severe gales blow in the southern summer, from December through March.

The advantage of long [summer] days is certainly very great, [wrote Captain Phillip Parker King in an early Cape Horn *Pilot*] but from my experience of the winds and weather . . . I preferred the winter passage, and in our subsequent experience of it, found no reason to alter my opinion. Easterly and northerly winds prevail in the winter off the cape, whilst southerly and westerly winds are constant during the summer months; and not only are the winds more favorable in the winter, but they are moderate in comparison to the fury of the summer gales.[32]

Since leaving Punta Arenas we hadn't seen a single person. Not a ship nor a fishing boat nor a distant man on horseback. All the Alacalufe, Ona, and Yaghan Indians that had amused and intrigued and plagued the early explorers and travelers were gone. No longer would a lone Joshua Slocum sprinkle carpet tacks on the deck of his yacht *Spray* to discourage unwanted visitors at night. The Indians had all vanished—except for a few—pathetic victims of disease, alcohol, a cruelly expanding white man's frontier, and a shattered culture. The handsome and skillful Onas who had lived by hunting the guanaco with bow and arrow had been decimated by tuberculosis and finally wiped out by measles. Margaret and I had seen a handful of Alacalufes in Puerto Edén further north, but they lived mostly on government handouts. We met one Yaghan in Puerto Williams. In reality, however, the Indians of Tierra del Fuego were extinct.

In the old days, the hardy, almost naked Alacalufes and Yaghans had lived in small dugouts or bark canoes and had traveled as nomads from place to place eating shellfish, a few wild plants, seal meat, and occasional blubber from a stranded whale. Each canoe always had a fire in the center, built over a thick bed of clay which served as both firebrick and ballast. Ashore the Indians lived in crude wigwams. Some writers called these people savages because they appeared to live scarcely better than animals. From Magellan in 1520 to Barclay in 1920, travelers' accounts are filled with stories of the canoe Indians who were filthy and greasy by European standards, but who somehow appeared to thrive in a very tough natural environment.

The Indians were seen on all the main islands and pas-

A Fuegian Indian at Puerto Williams on Isla Navarino. This aged survivor lived a simple and pleasant life and eked out his income by making model Yaghan canoes of the old style and selling them to occasional visitors.

sages and even on the most remote offshore islets. When James Weddell of the sealer *Jane of Leigh* anchored in remote St. Martin's cove on Isla Hermite in 1823 he was astonished to see Yaghans coming out to his brig. Soon the Indians were on board entertaining the sailors. Weddell was impressed by the Indians' ability to mimic the Englishmen:

A sailor had given a Fuegian a tin pot full of coffee which he drank, and was using all his art to steal the pot. The sailor, however, recollecting after a while that the pot had not been returned, applied for it, but whatever words he made use of were always repeated in imitation by the Fuegian. At length, he became enraged at hearing his requests reiterated, and placing himself in a threatening attitude, in an angry tone, he said, "You copper-coloured rascal, where is my tin pot?" The Fuegian, assuming the same attitude, with his eyes fixed on the sailor, called out "You copper-coloured rascal, where is my tin pot?" The imitation was so perfect, that every one laughed, except the sailor, who proceeded to search him, and under his arm he found the article missing.[33]

W. H. B. Webster explained how the Fuegians fished without metal or bone hooks: "They fasten a small limpet in its shell to the end of a line, which the fish readily swallows as bait. The greatest care is then taken by them not to displace the limpet from his stomach in drawing the fish gradually to the surface of the water; and when there, the woman watches a favourable moment, and with great dexterity, while she retains the fish by the line with one hand, seizes hold of it with the other and quickly lifts it into the canoe." [34]

Captain Charles Wilkes wrote from the Wollaston Islands in 1839:

We were here visited by a canoe with six natives, two old women, two young men, and two children. The two women were paddling, and the fire was burning in the usual place. They approached the vessel singing their rude song "Hey meh leh," and continued it until they came alongside. The expression of the younger ones was extremely prepossessing, evincing much intelligence and good humor. They ate ham and bread voraciously, distending their large mouths and showing a strong and beautiful set of teeth. A few strips of red flannel distributed among them produced great pleasure; they tied it around their heads as a sort of turban. Knowing they were fond of music, I had the fife played, the only instrument we could muster. They seemed much struck with the sound. The tune of "Yankee Doodle" they did not understand; but when "Bonnets of Blue" was played, they were all in motion keeping time to it. . . . I have seldom seen so happy a group. They were extremely lively and cheerful, and anything but miserable, if we could have avoided contrasting their condition with our own. The colour of the young men was a pale, and of the old a dark copper colour. Their heads were covered with ashes, but their exterior left a pleasing impression. Contentment was pictured in their countenances and actions, and produced a moral effect that will long be remembered.[35]

When Charles Darwin sailed on the *Beagle* he unwittingly made an observation that was to weigh heavily on the Indians' future. "In another harbour not far distant," he wrote, "a woman who was suckling a recently-born child, came alongside the vessel and remained there out of mere curiosity, whilst the sleet fell and thawed on her naked bosom, and on the skin of her naked baby." [36]

The indirect result of Darwin's remark was that tons of blankets and clothes were sent to the Indians. None of the writers or sailors or missionaries or anyone else realized that the Indians' oily skin quickly shed water. ("Indian's body all over like white man's face," noted Barclay too late.) No one considered that the Indians might be acutely susceptible to pulmonary diseases. Great efforts were made to Christianize the Indians and to get them to dress, live, and work like white men. It was all folly. When the Yaghans and Alacalufes and Onas wore damp clothes, the natives got chills that quickly turned to influenza, pneumonia, and consumption. Coupled with the problems of clothing was cultural interference. Once the Europeans began to tamper with the life styles of the Indians and to put them into settlements where they were obliged to learn such pointless idiocy as carpentry and sewing and Bible lessons, their reasons for living stopped.

Little Peter Duncan, once named Multgliunjer, may have learned about Jesus, but if Peter died of tuberculosis at age eleven, what was the use of the lessons if it deprived the child of his life? [37]

Lucas Bridges, who knew the Indians better than any other white man and spoke their language perfectly, visited a large group of Onas who were kept at a Silesian Christian mission on Dawson Island in 1900. Bridges's friend Hektliohlh had escaped from Ushuaia and had been captured once again by settlers and handed over to the Silesians.

"He looked with yearning towards the distant mountains of his native land," wrote Bridges. " 'Shouwe t-maten ya,' said Hektliohlh. ('Longing is killing me.')

"He did not survive very long," said Bridges. "Liberty is dear to white men; to untamed wanderers of the wilds it is an absolute necessity." [38]

It is easy to romanticize about the Indians who in fact became troublesome and thieving when white men began to spend time in the south. Even the most hardboiled sheep rancher, however, had to admit that the Indians' story was tragic and wretched.

We stopped at Puerto Fanny on Isla Stewart, Puerto Fortuna on Isla Londonderry, and at Caleta Voilier on Isla Gordon. Now *Whisper* was once again in Canal Beagle and we sailed past the six large glaciers that flowed down from the north side of the northwest arm of Beagle and discharged directly into the water. The winter snow lay deep on the mountains and we brushed against ice fragments in the channel. In one anchorage Margaret collected three buckets of mussels—of which there were thousands. Some of the mussels measured eight inches long. We kept them in water in the cockpit. At night the buckets froze solid and stayed frozen all day so the mussels were well refrigerated. We ate this batch of shellfish on and off for the next two weeks.

~~~~~~

Peruvian Mussel Soup

36 mussels
2 cups water
1 celery stalk with leaves (or dried celery)
2 tablespoons olive oil
1 medium onion, chopped or grated (or dried)
2 cloves garlic, crushed
1 teaspoon chili powder
1 tablespoon cornstarch
1 tablespoon chopped parsley (or dried parsley)
  Juice of ½ lemon
1 egg, beaten
1½ cups evaporated milk
  Salt and pepper to taste
  Fried croutons optional

• • •

Wash and scrub mussels. Place in large saucepan over high heat with water and celery until the mussels open. Remove mussels. Strain liquid through several thicknesses of cheesecloth. Extract mussels from shells.

Heat oil in saucepan and fry onion, garlic, and chili powder. Add mussel liquid and bring to a boil; add cornstarch mixed with 2 tablespoons water. Bring to a boil and simmer 8 to 10 minutes. Take pot from fire, add mussels, parsley, and lemon juice. Mix egg and milk and gradually add to soup. Stir thoroughly and heat but do not boil. Season to taste. Serve with fried croutons. Enough for 3–4 people or 2 hungry sailors.

~~~~~~

One thing a shipwreck impresses on you indelibly is the need for instant action. On July 26 we were asleep at Caleta Sonia during a light snowfall. Suddenly the motion of the vessel was different. I was wide awake. The wind had changed to the east and we were straining at our cable on a lee shore.

We never dressed quicker in our life. In two or three minutes Margaret and I were on deck looking over the situation and ready to move or to put out another anchor. We were bumping slightly on a shallow near a small islet a few hundred feet east of the Yamana lighthouse. We had one hundred thirty feet of chain out, but with the change in wind we had swung into only six feet of depth. I winched in thirty-five feet of chain a little at a time as we lifted on passing swells. We eased into deeper water and headed more into the wind and rode easier. We stood anchor watches until daybreak when we moved to an adjoining bay with better protection. Here I hoped to anchor in twelve or fifteen feet, but even though I watched the plow anchor drop on clean sand the anchor failed to bite in. It took four tries before I was satisfied. Again and again in the channels we found that shallow anchoring was a fraud. We finally got well set in a depth of forty feet with two hundred feet of chain out while we waited for the east wind to change.

When the wind relented we sailed eastward along Canal Beagle. Margaret had washed out some red thermal underwear and had hung it on the lifelines to dry. The underwear froze hard enough to stand up by itself, so we propped it up in a corner of the cockpit to keep the helmsman company. East of Caleta Sonia we passed five black and white killer whales heading westward. One had an extremely tall dorsal fin. On earlier trips we had seen these wide-ranging mammals in the Galápagos Islands and on the west coast of Vancouver Island. The small whales never paid any attention to us.

Two days later we glided into the Chilean navy base at Puerto Williams where we tied up near the *Castor*, the navy workboat that had helped to pull *Whisper* from the beach when she was wrecked. It was marvelous to see Lieutenant Horacio Balmelli and Bosun Oluf Torres and the rest of the crew again and to show them our newly repaired vessel which certainly looked happier than the patched hulk they had hauled off the beach in the Wollaston Islands.

One morning when I was carrying a box of groceries to the yacht a navy truck stopped. "Hop in," said the friendly

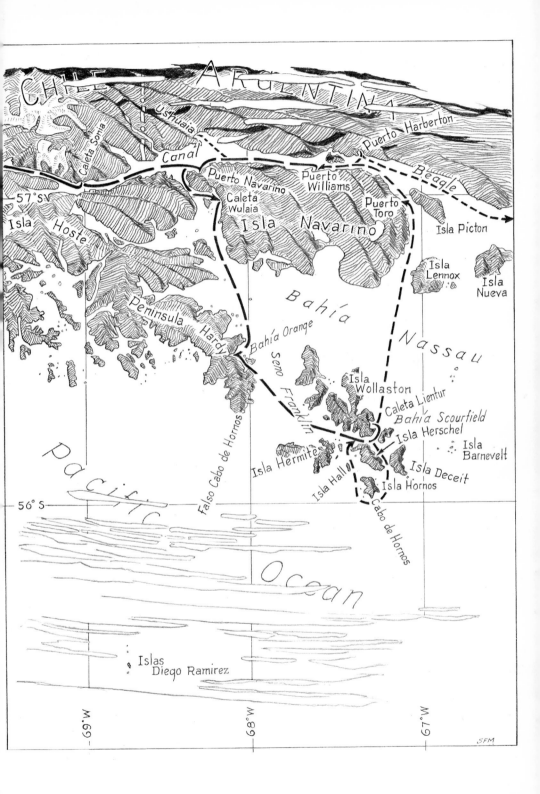

driver. "I'm going down to the dock." I got in and we roared off. The driver had a radio going full blast, he was eating a cheese sandwich, and he was talking nonstop. Unfortunately he was so occupied that he failed to watch a turn in the road and the truck bounced off the track, tore down a row of small trees, and lurched into a ditch. The driver was astonished but he continued to eat his cheese sandwich while the radio blared away. We crawled out of the truck whose starboard wheels were spinning in the air. People came running from all directions and soon had the truck back on the

We arrived at the Chilean naval base of Puerto Williams on Isla Navarino on a beautiful sunny afternoon after a good sail along Canal Beagle. That night, however, a blizzard blew up and in the morning Puerto Williams had a heavy frosting of snow.

road. I had banged one knee hard against the dashboard, but I recovered my box of groceries and limped off down the road, swearing to stay away from dangerous automobiles and trucks which obviously were much more lethal than the risks of Cape Horn.

In the evening Margaret and I walked up to the officers' club where we saw some of our friends. "I feel very humiliated because of my blunder that caused the wreck," I said to a group of Chilean officers.

"Relax," said one of the men. "It was bad luck. Down here we all need divine help to stay out of trouble. Why everyone in this room has been wrecked in the channels at one time or another."

Another man interrupted. "That's wrong," he said with a sympathetic smile. "I've been shipwrecked twice."

We had coffee, much pleasant talk about a dozen subjects, and were given valuable information about anchorages near Cape Horn. The evening was marvelous, but as we walked along the frosty track on the way back to the yacht, I couldn't help comparing my afternoon truck ride with the pleasurable evening, and to speculate on the Chilean character. I thought of the contrast between my frustrations during the repairs at the Asmar shipyard in Punta Arenas in the daytime working hours, and of the many delightful social occasions with the hospitable Chileans during the evenings. The Chileans were certainly not methodical planners nor a punctual, mechanically inclined race, but a people who somehow muddled along in the business world with a different sense of values. I had learned about their carefully prepared, beautifully served meals, their readiness to please, and their cordial manners. If I needed an engineer or a business analyst I would hire a German or a Swiss. But if I wanted a person with the ultimate in charm, a captivating manner, and the height of refinement, I would pick a Chilean. Who else would be an hour late for an important luncheon engagement because he stopped to select and arrange a bouquet of flowers for the hostess?

Just as I was writing this and was worried that I might insult my Chilean friends who had been so helpful and generous there was a great bang on deck. I looked out to see a big chunk of meat on the side deck.

"I just thought you would like half a lamb," said Lieutenant Balmelli. "We have plenty more if you need it."

From Puerto Williams we sailed south through Canal Murray. The mountain scenery rose up on all sides and looked doubly dramatic in the long winter dawn and dusk when the pale, low-angled rays from the sun cast pink and purple light on the snow and clouds and granite crests. A big condor flew overhead, its wingtip feathers flexing and opening with each slow beat. We anchored at Caleta Wulaia at the west end of the Isla Navarino. Ashore we saw a two-story yellow building with a red tin roof and windows trimmed in green with a black iron balcony on the north side. Presumably we were at a sheep ranch because of the outbuildings and fences and facilities for handling animals. But not a person nor a sign of anyone. What a difference from April 1830 when Mr. Murray from the *Beagle* discovered this channel and the broad east–west canal to the north that would be named after his ship.

Murray saw upward of a hundred canoes in one day, each containing from two to six people. The Fuegians had many guanaco skins, and some of the bones of the animals had been made into spearheads. The Indians appeared to be tractable and less disposed to quarreling than those further west, noted Murray. Wherever the whaleboat from the *Beagle* went she was followed by a train of the canoes, each full of people, and each with a fire smoking in the middle of the frail canoe.[39]

By 1859, it is sad to say, relations between the white men and Indians had deteriorated to such a point that the Yaghans murdered eight men of a missionary party whose vessel, the *Allen Gardiner*, had been anchored right where *Whisper* now swung so easily in the sunlight.

"Did you hear a knock?" I said to Margaret.

"A knock?" she replied.

(Overleaf) In rough water south of Isla Navarino.

"Yes. A knock from the ghosts of those missionaries," I said.[40]

We were only sixty miles from Cape Horn. The next stop was Caleta Misión in Bahía Orange on Península Hardy. The Chilean navy had asked us to check in at various lookout stations in the southern waters. There were always two men, a radioman and a gunner, who were sent out for several months to keep an eye on an area and to radio in weather information. We had shown our clearances to the lookouts in Canal Murray and now we headed for Caleta Misión. We arrived late in the day during a heavy snowstorm, anchored, and rowed ashore to meet Juan Cordova and Luis Sespedes, two astonished young naval ratings who had seen no one else for several months. They had little to do except to cook for each other and to exercise the dogs. The gunner oiled his weapons and the radioman tapped out daily reports by morse code on a 1940 U.S. radio set. The two sailors told us that at the beginning of July the wind had blown from the west at

These two smiling Chilean navy ratings maintained the lookout station at Bahía Orange.

140 kilometers per hour (70 knots or 85 mph) *for seven days without stopping*. Both men were so pleased to see us—or anyone—that they would hardly let us leave, but we wanted to get to a recommended anchorage west of Isla Yellow before dark. Before we left we walked up to see a bronze plaque that commemorated the 1882–83 French scientific expedition under the command of Louis Martial. The light was already fading in the thickly falling snow when we rowed away from the little dock at Caleta Misión while the men waved good-bye.

On August 6 I sluiced down the decks with buckets of seawater to wash away the snow while Margaret winched up the mainsail. Once underway we headed southeast toward the complex of Islas Wollaston, Hermite, Herschel, and Hornos that lay strong on the horizon. The sky was blue, a yellowish sun was rising off the port bow, and we had a fair northwest wind of fifteen knots. We eased the mainsail, poled out a jib, and hurried toward our goal, once again feeling the swell of the Southern Ocean. Behind us the snowy mountains above Bahía Schapenham on Peninsula Hardy glinted so brightly in the flat light that my eyes could hardly stand the glare.

Though many outlying parts of the world were discovered by the English, Spanish, and Portuguese, it was the resourceful and practical Dutch who first saw the islands before us. In 1616 the 360-ton Dutch ship *Unitie* under the command of Willem Schouten slipped between the easternmost point of Tierra del Fuego and a mountainous island to the east. The Dutch named the strait Le Maire for one of the expedition's leaders; the island was called Staten Island after the States General, the governing body of Holland. On January 29, 1616, while sailing southwest, the *Unitie* passed a high snow-covered islet which ended in a point that was named De Cap Hoorn, after Schouten's home city of Hoorn, Holland. De Cap Hoorn, corrupted to Cape Horn (or Cabo de Hornos in Spanish), soon became famous because it was the troublesome dividing point between voyages in the Atlantic

The snowy peaks above Bahía Schapenham shone golden in the morning sun as we headed south and east with one reef tied in the mainsail.

In Bahía Orange we washed the snow off Whisper's decks with buckets of sea water.

and the Pacific. Cape Horn often meant dreadful weather, discomfort, cold, and sickness, and marked the low point of long and arduous voyages.[41]

Now more than three hundred fifty years later, we sped to the southeast with a freshening wind that backed to the north as we neared the islands. By noon we were in Seno Franklin and approaching Isla Herschel with the mountains of Isla Hermite to starboard. The wind increased to thirty-five knots in Canal Franklin, and with the mainsail down we reached along at a great clip while we checked off point after point on the chart. As we passed the east end of Hermite and several small islets we suddenly had a clear line of vision to the south.

We could see Isla Hall—a rocky summit that rose impressively from the ocean—and *Isla Hornos itself*. Heavens! Here was Cape Horn at last. The famous cape on the south face was in plain sight even from our viewpoint to the north-northwest. If it hadn't been so late in the day we could have sailed around the island.

A few minutes later our view of Cape Horn was cut off by Isla Herschel. Ahead we saw a Chilean motor torpedo boat to which we dipped our national flag and received a similar signal in return. An hour later we exchanged Aldis lamp signals with the Chilean lookout station at the northeast corner of Herschel. I had worked out a simplistic message in Spanish which I dot-dashed to the radio operator. The rapid-fire blinking light that came back quite overwhelmed my modest mastery of morse, especially in Spanish abbreviations, so I signaled OK to whatever had been sent and we hurried to Caleta Lientur on the northwest side of Bahía Scourfield, another seven miles. Two dozen small seals followed us into the anchorage and played around *Whisper*, leaping out of the water again and again. As we sailed into the bay a squadron of steamer ducks flapped off toward the far shore, their wings and feet making a great commotion as they fled before us.

The weather was going to hell. The darkening sky looked

nasty. Low clouds with ragged bottoms rapidly blew toward us and the wind began to gust strongly. We were soon well set in Caleta Lientur, but the poor yacht heeled first to the right and then to the left as terrific squalls poured down from the mountains of Isla Wollaston. During the night I heard a sail flapping and I rushed on deck to discover that the force of the squalls had somehow blown all the sail ties to the end of the main boom and had allowed the mainsail to escape. Though we were close to a weather shore the violence of the williwaws was enough to fling spray over the entire yacht.

Our salvation during those months in the south was our Dickinson diesel stove which kept the interior of the yacht warm and dry and pleasant. This well-made metal stove measured eighteen by twenty by twenty-two inches and weighed 119 pounds. Its silent pot burner used about one gallon of kerosene or diesel oil every twenty-four hours fed from a gravity tank. Margaret was able to bake four loaves of bread at a time in the oven and usually kept two kettles of water on the back of the stove for hot drinks and for washing.

The westerly gale lasted two and a half days. My journal for August 7 read:

1900 Suddenly the wind is gone. Everything is calm and we hear only the tinkling of water along the hull. It is quiet for a minute, two minutes. Then a low moaning starts in the distance. The noise increases rapidly and climbs higher in pitch as the squall comes closer. I peer out with a flashlight. All is black and the only thing I can see are horizontal streaks of snow. The wind shrieks and a spiraling blast lashes the vessel which shakes like a bundle of rags in the jaws of a playful dog.

I time the wind. Now it is calm (19:11). I hear the wind coming (19:13). Now more quickly (19:13:15). The wind is on us and we heel to 20, 30, 40 degrees (19:14). A line beats against the mast. Water splashes from a kettle on the hot stove and I hear a hiss of steam. I grab the wind indicator, push back the hatch, and rush outside to measure the wind. The red disc flies to the top of the scale. 63 knots. The cold is terrible. I slam the hatch, shake the snow from my hair, and run to the stove. The wind flails at the yacht. All at once the hurricane blast is gone. Again we hear only the tinkling of water along the hull.

It was the sound of the wind that got to me after a while. The continual moaning. The crescendos. The hollow roar. The scream when it was on us. But these words are meaningless because they merely describe the edge of the wind. No one can talk about the squalls of Cape Horn. You must experience their color and shape and size and intensity yourself.

On the morning of August 9 the storm was over. At 0730 we looked out into the clear winter sky and saw Venus, Orion, and the Southern Cross shining brightly in the dawn. We got underway at once. Two hours later we were between Isla Herschel and Isla Deceit, sailing southbound with a single-reefed mainsail and a working jib that pulled us along nicely in a twenty-knot easterly breeze. We passed around an islet off the eastern tip of Herschel. Isla Hornos lay about four miles in front of us to the southwest.

The bleak island was five miles long and two miles wide, with its major dimension on a northwest–southeast line. The land was well elevated above the water and looked somewhat flat and saddle-shaped with a low hill at the northwest end. As we sailed along the east side of the island we saw clumps of beech trees and patches of shrubs. My friend Eugene Anthony, who visited the island in 1974 with the Chilean navy, told me that there were many traces of Indian camping places, no doubt the same type that Margaret and I had found when we camped in the Wollaston Islands twenty-four miles to the north.

I had read about two marginal anchorages on the east side; we had planned to stop and to go ashore for a firsthand look at this fantastic place. Through the binoculars, however, I saw breaking swells all along the eastern side. With the

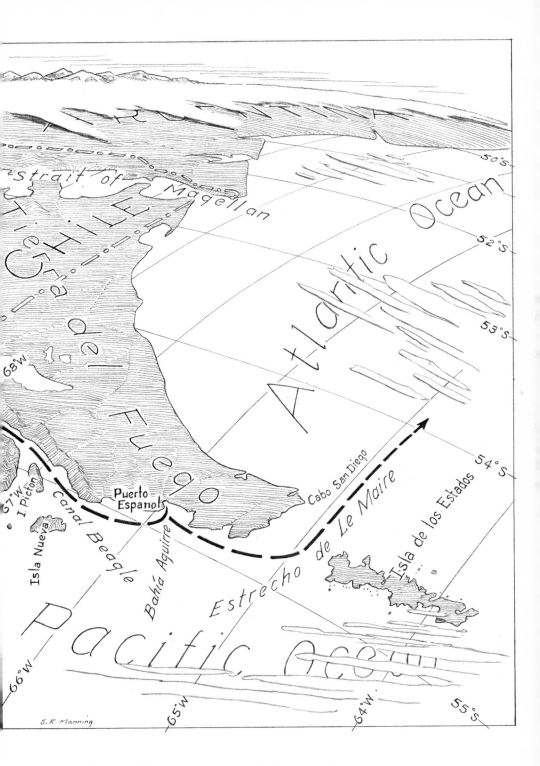

On the map:

CHILE

Strait of Magellan

Atlantic Ocean

50°S

52°S

53°S

54°S

55°S

68°W

Tierra de

Fuego

67°W
I. Picton

Isla Nueva

Canal Beagle

Puerto Español

Bahía Aguirre

Cabo San Diego

Estrecho de Le Maire

Isla de los Estados

Pacific Ocean

66°W

65°W

64°W

S. E. Manning

*(Overleaf) View south across Isla Herschel. The snowy summit
of Cape Horn rises just above Herschel.*

wind from the eastern quadrant the anchorages were impossible.

As we sailed briskly along, all eyes turned to starboard as the south face of the island opened up. We watched Isla Hornos climb to its highest point—1,331 feet—and we looked at the triangular, pointed cliff that tumbled into the Southern Ocean amidst a jagged horror of black rocks and snow and upset water.

I gasped as I looked. Could this be it at last? Cape Horn? I let out a Texas yell. "Yippee! We made her!" I shook my hands over my head, smiled at Margaret, and did a little dance down the port side deck.

"Quick! Write it in the log before you fall over the side," shouted Margaret.

No lightning and thunder clapped down from Zeus. No meteors fell out of the sky. Yet it was a milestone for us to sail our toy boat to Cape Horn via the intricate Chilean waterways with their savage winds. By the time we got to the east coast of the United States we would have sailed twenty thousand miles from California. On the voyage we had had plenty of sail drill, anchoring, the wreck, the salvage, the repair, and the Cape Horn winter run. An intriguing experience. I grew serious and thought of all our friends in the U.S., Peru, and Chile who had helped us. And the wonderful assistance from the navy of Chile when we had been blown ashore. I turned and looked at Margaret— the world's keenest traveler—with affection.

We swung around Isla Hornos toward Isla Hall and as we did a frigid north wind headed us. I thought of the Chilean joke about sailing: "Yes, the wind always blows from the bow." We made our way back to Caleta Lientur, and by stages to Navarino Island where we cleared for Argentina. We sailed to Ushuaia and tied up next to Vasko Arregui's fishboat *Cruz del Sur* and were introduced to the *centolla* or spider king crab, the world's most delicious food. We stopped at Harberton and Puerto Español on the Argentine

FINAL TRIUMPH

coast of Tierra del Fuego.

When the barometer was high and steady we sailed for the Strait of Le Maire, the great meeting point of the Atlantic and Pacific, where tidal overfalls have capsized large ships. We arranged to be at the strait exactly at slack water as recommended. Yet the seas were awful, simply horrendous, and we had the added zest of a southwest gale that erupted from nowhere and soon enclosed us in a swirling blizzard. Sailing blind and committed to the strait because

Margaret and her friend, Vasko Arregui, with a spider king crab.

(Overleaf) Cape Horn from the southwest.

of the gale, we rushed through Le Maire at four knots under bare pole with no sails up at all. The seas were enough to make the strong weep, and we had to steer like dinghy sailors to keep from broaching. We knew the wind was strong because the tops of the seas were blown off in streaks of white spume.

But the strait was short and soon we were in the South Atlantic with a weather shore and unlimited sea room. No more would we be obliged to anchor under those mountains and to feel the blasts of the hurricane squalls. No longer would we have ninety-minute anchor drills every morning and evening. I was sick to death of our snail-like progress during the seven or eight hours of winter daylight. I was weary of the intricate pilotage. Now it was all behind us. As we edged our way to the northeast from Isla de los Estados it was grand to feel the regular swells of the South Atlantic.

Once away from land we began to see the familiar brown and white checkered mantles of pintado petrels and the never-ending circling and swooping of black-browed and wandering albatrosses.

We looked at a wandering albatross with disbelief. This great white clown of fluff and feathers that peered down on us across his yellowish bill had a wingspan of fourteen feet. Fourteen feet? Any bird that size was an invention of the mind. A humorous fantasy. But the whole Cape Horn region was a land of wonders and exaggeration, a myth of hyperbole and high coloring. I was Baron Munchausen. I was Aesop. I was Alice in Wonderland. I had dreamed the whole trip.

Whether indeed it was a vapor of the mind or something more factual, the flinty reality of Cape Horn and the channels of Chile was behind us. We had accomplished our goals: a transit of the waterways, a sail in the Strait of Magellan, and a close look at the Tierra del Fuego and Cape Horn. In ninety-seven anchorages and 2,438 miles of sailing between Canal Chacao and Isla de los Estados we had seen another marvelous slice of the wild places on our wonderful planet.

(Overleaf) Headed northward in the Strait of Le Maire between Tierra del Fuego and Isla de los Estados. A southwest storm is behind us and the wind is strong enough so that we are going along at four knots under bare pole without any sail up at all. This strait is the meeting ground for vast quantities of water from the Pacific and Atlantic and is a most hazardous place. We arrived exactly at slack water but found simply horrendous seas. Fortunately it took only a few hours to sail through Le Maire Strait and out into the comparative safety of the South Atlantic.

281

Notes

1. William Albert Robinson, *To the Great Southern Sea* (London: Peter Davies, 1957).
2. Antonio Pigafetta, *The Voyage of Magellan,* trans. Paula Spurlin Paige (Englewood Cliffs, N.J.: Prentice-Hall, 1969), pp. 19–23.
3. Yves Le Scal, *The Great Days of the Cape Horners* (New York: The New American Library, 1967). This excellent and intriguing book was first published in France under the title *La grand épopée des Cap-Horniers* and is based on the papers of Captain Henri Briend who both commanded Cape Horn ships and gathered reminiscences from twenty-nine Cape Horn masters. The book is particularly valuable because of the overview of world shipping and the role of sail and steam from 1849 to 1914. Also see Raymond A. Rydell, *Cape Horn to the Pacific* (Berkeley: University of California Press, 1952), a general summary with remarkable references.
4. This brief sketch of Al Hansen is based on an interview and photographs in *La Prensa* (Buenos Aires) dated February 18, 1934. Also from recollections of Bobby Uriburu given to the author on January 12, 1969, and a letter dated April 29, 1975. In addition, I have a letter from Germán Frers Sr. dated April 19, 1977, a photograph given to me by Manolo Campos, and a letter from Mr. S. Lyngaas of the Norwegian Government Directorate for Seamen in Oslo dated February 9, 1977. A good summary is by D. H. Clarke, *An Evolution of Single-handers* (London: Stanford Maritime, 1975), p. 121. The three famous Argentine sailors—Bobby Uriburu, Germán Frers Sr., and Vito Dumas—all got acquainted with Hansen

when he stopped in Buenos Aires. It was from this meeting that Dumas conceived the idea for his great voyage of 1942–43. There is a marvelous 1934 photograph of Hansen and Dumas together in Dumas's book *Los Cuarenta Bramadores* (Buenos Aires: Editorial Atlantida S.A., 1944), p. 12. According to a 1934 story in the *South Pacific Mail*, the American wife of Mr. Hansen, Mrs. Mary Jane Hansen, was living close to Boston, Massachusetts.

5. Miles Smeeton, *Because the Horn Is There* (Sidney, British Columbia, Canada: Gray's Publishing, 1971), pp. 86–87.

6. John Brooks, ed., *The 1975 South American Handbook* (Bath England: Trade & Travel), p. 345; *Columbia Encyclopedia*, 3rd ed., pp. 333 & 401.

7. Francisco A. Encina, *Historia de Chile* (Santiago: Editorial Nascimento, 1952), 5:61.

8. Charles Darwin, *The Voyage of the Beagle*, edited by Leonard Engel (New York: Doubleday, 1962), p. 52.

9. Bernardo Quintana Mansilla, *Chiloé Mitológico*, Propiedad Intelectual (Chile), no. 39985, June 21, 1972.

10. H. W. Tilman, *Mischief in Patagonia* (Cambridge: University Press, 1957), p. 102; also see Rae Natalie Prosser de Goodall, *Tierra del Fuego* (Buenos Aires: Foundation of the Banco Francés del Rio de la Plata, 1970), p. 22.

11. Leo Heaps, *Log of the Centurian* (New York: Macmillan, 1973), pp. 25, 116. This book is based on the recent discovery of the Saumarez logbooks and gives new information on Anson's voyage. On page 117 is a crude map drawn by someone on board the *Anna* which sketches Bahía Anna Pink together with four tiny drawings of the vessel which shows the *Anna* rigged as a bark. It is obvious that the first island the *Anna* tried to anchor behind was Isla Inchemo, not in the Inchin group as has been written elsewhere. The best-known account of Anson's voyage was written by his chaplain, Richard Walter, *A Voyage Around the World* (London: J. M. Dent, 1911), pp. 130–138. A few details differ from the Heaps book.

12. Charles Darwin, *Voyage*, pp. 284–285 (quoted by the editor, Leonard Engel, from Fitz Roy).

13. Philip Davenport, *The Voyage of 'Waltzing Matilda'* (London: Hutchinson, 1953), p. 85.

14. Walter, *A Voyage*, This 1911 edition has a marvelous twelve-page introduction by John Masefield who ably sketches the ships and men of Anson's era. Also see John Bulkeley and

John Cummins, *A Voyage to the South Seas* (New York: McBride, 1927); Richard Hough, *The Blind Horn's Hate* (New York: Norton, 1971); S. W. C. Pack, *The Wager Mutiny* (London: Alvin Redman, 1964), the best and most balanced account of a complex story. The crew list and totals of survivors at different times varies from account to account and perhaps never will be known accurately.

15. Samuel Eliot Morison, *The European Discovery of America, The Southern Voyages* A.D. *1492–1616* (New York: Oxford, 1974), the outstanding one-volume digest of all the early voyages. Also see Admiral Don A. De Cordova, *A Voyage of Discovery to the Strait of Magellan* . . . (London: Richard Phillips, 1789?).

16. Joshua Slocum, *Sailing Alone Around the World* (Westvaco Corporation, 1969), p. 125. Slocum's writing about the Strait of Magellan and Cockburn Channel is so accurate that his book can be used as a *Pilot*. Every bit of his voyage can be retraced. Louis Bernicot, *The Voyage of Anahita* (London: Rupert Hart-Davis, 1953), p. 76. A simple sparse book, but one of my favorites. I have always been amazed at how Captain Bernicot contrived to cut and sew new sails inside his small cabin while underway on the ocean.

17. *South America Pilot* (London: Hydrographic Department, Admiralty, 1956), 2:25.

18. Louis de Bougainville, *A Voyage Round the World*, Bibliotheca Australiana #12 (New York: Da Capo Press, 1967), p. 188, a recent reprint of the 1772 English edition.

19. Morison, *European Discovery*, p. 647; Felix Riesenberg *Cape Horn* (New York: Dodd, Mead, 1939), p. 59. Captain Riesenberg is chatty and informative but not as thorough or accurate as Morison. Riesenberg's conjecture about Drake's vanished island is fascinating. Well worth reading for general information.

20. Morison, *European Discovery*, pp. 690–717; Hough, *Blind Horn's Hate*, p. 108; Riesenberg, *Cape Horn*, pp. 96–104; W. S. Barclay, *The Land of Magellan* (London: Methuen, 1926), p. 63.

21. Morison, *European Discovery*, p. 401.

22. Willy de Roos, a Dutchman living in Belgium, sailed *Williwaw*, a 42-foot steel ketch. Sometimes de Roos sailed alone but usually with crew. Tom Zydler, a Pole who now lives in the United States, was the captain of the *Konstanty Maciejewicz*, a 45-foot wooden yawl which had five aboard, includ-

ing a woman psychiatrist. Both passed through the Strait of
Magellan in 1973.

23. Slocum, *Sailing Alone*, p. 106.

24. *South America Pilot*, 2:164.

25. R. W. Coppinger, *Cruise of the Alert* (London: Swan Sonnen-
schein, 1899), p. 37.

26. Yves Le Scal, *Great Days*, pp. 31–32.

27. Charles Wilkes, *Narrative of the United States Exploring Expedition* . . . (Philadelphia: Lea and Blanchard, 1845), p. 145;
W. Parker Snow, *A Two Years' Cruise off Tierra del Fuego*
. . . (2 vols.; London: Longman, Brown, Green, Longmans,
& Roberts, 1857), 2:57–64.

28. L.-F. Martial, *Mission Scientifique du Cap Horn*, (Paris:
Gauthier-Villars, 1888), 1:234; Rockwell Kent, *Voyaging
Southward from the Strait of Magellan* (New York: G. P.
Putnam, 1924), p. 163.

29. Bougainville, *Round the World*, p. 159.

30. Lloyd Hirst, *Coronel and After* (London: Peter Davies,
1934); Riesenberg, *Cape Horn*, pp. 376–382; *Columbia Encyclopedia*, 3rd ed., p. 2016; Oliver Warner, *Great Sea Battles*
(New York: Macmillan, 1963), p. 253.

31. *Narrative of the Surveying Voyages of His Majesty's Ships
Adventure and Beagle* . . . (4 vols.; London: Henry Colburn,
1839), 1:388–392. These three volumes (plus one of notes
and tables) are the best source of channel life in the nineteenth century. Excellent, absorbing stuff. Regrettably, the
volumes are rare items.

32. Phillip Parker King, *Sailing Directions for the Coasts of Eastern and Western Patagonia* (London: Hydrographic Office,
Admiralty, 1832), p. 140; Martial, *Mission*, p. 244. This
French officer, who spent two years at Bahía Orange, also
urges westbound travel in the winter because the winds are
more favorable, the weather is less bad, and there are fewer
chances of damage to the ships. Patrick Van God, *Trismus*
(Paris: B. Arthaud, 1974), p. 105. The text of this present-
day yachtsman, recently reported lost, includes the comments
of Captain Pedro Margalot concerning weather in the south.

33. James Weddell, *A Voyage Towards the South Pole* (London:
Longman, Hurst, Rees, Orme, Brown, and Green, 1825), p.
154; for a hair-raising account of a sailor's experiences with
southern Indians, see Benjamin Franklin Bourne, *The Captive
in Patagonia* (Boston: Gould and Lincoln, 1853).

34. W. H. B. Webster, *Narrative of a Voyage to the Southern*

Atlantic Ocean (London: Richard Bentley, 1834), 1:182.

35. Wilkes, *Narrative,* p. 142.

36. Darwin, *Voyage,* p. 213.

37. Kent, *Voyaging Southward,* p. 158; Eric Shipton, *Tierra del Fuego: The Fatal Lodestone* (London: Charles Knight, 1973), p. 105; Barclay, *Land of Magellan,* p. 130.

38. E. Lucas Bridges, *Uttermost Part of the Earth* (London: Hodder and Stoughton, 1948), p. 267; Armando Braun Menendez, *Chroniques Australes* (Paris: Gallimard, 1961), pp. 163–260; John W. Marsh and W. H. Stirling, *The Story of Commander Allen Gardiner* (London: James Nisbet, 1874). In my opinion the full story of the Indians of Tierra del Fuego still remains to be written. The accounts I have seen are entirely too kind to the missionaries. W. Parker Snow, the first captain of the *Allen Gardiner,* has been quite ignored, as has the aspect of land taken from the natives and used for sheep ranching. Reduced to one sentence, the poor Indians were simply in the way of the white man's expanding frontier and could not cope either physically or mentally.

39. *Narrative of the Surveying Voyages of His Majesty's Ships Adventure and Beagle,* 1:429.

40. Bridges, *Uttermost Part,* pp. 43–45.

41. Morison, *European Discovery,* chap. 31; Hendrik Willem van Loon, *The Golden Book of the Dutch Navigators* (New York: Century Co., 1916), pp. 279–300.